STRONG CHURCH FOUNDATIONS

Building people into the Local Church

Colin J. Cooper

STRONG CHURCH FOUNDATIONS

Colin J. Cooper

Huddersfield Christian Fellowship

Copyright © 2010 Cathedral House Media

The author asserts the moral right to be identified as the author of this work in accordance with the Copyright, Design and Patents Act 1988

Cover Design and Layout by Marcus Woolcock

Published & Distributed by:

Integrity Media Europe

Hargreaves Business Park

Hargreaves Road

Eastbourne

East Sussex

BN23 6QW

UK

www.integrityprovident.co.uk

ISBN: 978-1-907080-14-2

First Edition 2010

Acknowledgements

Scripture quotations are taken from the New International Version® 1973, 1978, 1984 International Bible Society. Used by permission of Zondervan. All rights reserved. Scripture quotations marked AV are from the Holy Bible, King James Version (Authorized Version). First published in 1611. Used by permission of Zondervan. All rights reserved.

A catalogue record for this book is available from the British Library

DEDICATION

This book is dedicated to my wife Sue, who has been an inspiration, a friend and an incredible help throughout the writing of this book.

I would like to thank Keith Bond who is a faithful member of Huddersfield Christian Fellowship. Keith typed the pages and corrected the grammar, which took many hours of his time.

I also appreciate very much Celia Goldsmith, Basia Armitage, Anthony Green and Sue Bond along with my wife Sue for proof-reading this script.

This book would not have been possible without the support of the members of Huddersfield Christian Fellowship who worship in Cathedral House.

Finally, this book would not have been written had I not had an encounter with Jesus. This was made possible through John McKale who boldly approached me in the street and introduced me to Jesus Christ.

INTRODUCTION

Today, many individuals do not have a full grasp of the Church. Some regard the Church as a club that they can join to fulfil their needs and then leave when it no longer satisfies their desires. Others even treat the Church like an old cloth that they can discard when they have finished using it.

So in effect, there are many well-meaning, but misguided, believers who do not have a very solid foundation of Church and of what the Church actually is.

This book is more of a manual to give believers and non-believers a basic grasp of the awesome plan and purpose of the organism called the Church. This book has been designed to give Pastors, Teachers and Leaders a tool to help each person, whether a member or a potential member, to understand something of the mind of God concerning Church. The principles that are explained in this book are not just a theory, but have a proven track record of building people into Church so they become effective members who find their place in the Body of Christ. The principles given are solidly backed by scripture and have been fruitful in building Church.

To help each student, an occasional blank space has been left for them to fill in to give them a better opportunity to remember some key phrases. Each answer has been given at the back of the book to help the teachers in their research and to assist students when comparing their own answers.

My desire is for Leaders to use this proven method for building a healthy Church. I sincerely hope that all who are taught from this book will reach their God-intended purpose.

Church is the greatest organism on the Earth today, and I am sure that after the lessons have been understood, believers will grasp this fact and walk for a long period of time enjoying each other's company and finding fulfilment in the House of the Lord.

Psalm 27:4
"One thing I ask of the Lord, this is what I seek, that I may dwell in the House of the Lord all the days of my life, to gaze upon the beauty of the Lord and to seek Him in His temple."

Colin J. Cooper
Senior Pastor
Huddersfield Christian Fellowship
www.huddersfieldchristianfellowship.com

STRONG CHURCH FOUNDATIONS
Building people into the Local Church

CONTENTS

CHAPTER 1
MAKING DISCIPLES

1. MAKING DISCIPLES

One of the last commands Jesus gave us was to go into all the world and make disciples (Matt. 28:18-20). This is a principle that has been lost to the Church for some time, yet it is one of the great commands. But what exactly is a disciple?

The Greek word *mathetes* means 'a learner', from the verb *manthano*, 'to learn'. Often in Church, if a person has knowledge, we mistake it for maturity, but the Bible says the opposite is true (1 Cor. 8:1). Knowledge_____.

> Bible College is not actually found in the Bible, but was founded when the Church had lost its way in the period called 'The Dark Age of the Church'. Bible College students receive information, but not Life.

Correct attitudes lead to correct handling of knowledge (Phil. 2:5).

A.   New Christians love God (1 Cor. 8:3), but in time they know only scripture. The man who_____ God is known by God, rather than the man who knows scripture.

B.   Most adults give the impression they know a little about everything, or give the appearance that they know more than they actually do. Society has much more knowledge, but it has not been taught to learn.
Jesus said, "Make_____" (Matt. 28:19).
Charles Simpson said, "I would rather teach a man how to learn than teach him all I know."

SOCIETY LOOKS FOR ABILITY – BUT GOD LOOKS FOR RIGHT CHARACTER

A. A head full of scriptures does not necessarily indicate a godly person: he might just have a trained brain. Even a parrot can be taught to repeat scriptures.

B. A man that can be corrected loves knowledge, but the one who hates correction is_____ (Prov. 12:1).

C. Let the wise teach? – no, this is not what the Bible says, but rather, let the wise_____ and add to their learning (Prov. 1:5).

D. Instruct a wise man and he will be_____ still (Prov. 9:9), or the wise make good disciples as they are teachable.

HOW CAN WE TELL EARTHLY WISDOM FROM HEAVENLY WISDOM?

A. Heavenly wisdom is the opposite of all earthly wisdom (James 3:13-18).

B. It is possible to be right, yet very wrong. All depends on the attitude behind it. When the Pharisees came to Jesus, He did not tell them they were wrong, but called them 'hypocrites' and 'whitewashed tombs' (Matt. 23:27). They had knowledge of the scriptures, but said it with wrong attitudes.

SYMPTOMS OF AN UNTEACHABLE SPIRIT

1. Opinionated people rarely keep friends. They_____ in airing their own opinions (Prov. 18:2).

2. They love to talk about their experiences. Don't_____ to be somebody (Prov. 12:9).

3. They are not good listeners, but would rather talk and give answers, before they listen (Prov. 18:13).

4. They cannot receive_____ easily, but are defensive (Prov. 13:13).

5. The unteachable will throw up other issues to cloud the one at hand.

6. They constantly undermine those Leaders over them, and often try to see decisions reversed. Like Korah, they are often respected community Leaders (Num. 16; Jude 11).

7. Dealing with problems in the lives of the unteachable can be difficult as they often

ask for more definitions and examples: they ask, "What do you mean?" when the problem is crystal clear.

8.   The unteachable know better and want to be the_____ instead of the disciple.

9.   After long arguments, they will back away due to tiredness, but return again the following week, still arguing.

10.   They are always looking for an alternative explanation to the one given.

11.   When corrected, they feel victimised and wonder, "Why is it always me?"

12.   People need them, but they do not need others.

13.   Unteachable people feel they are always a special case.

14.   When things do not go their way, they show annoyance and get depressed.

15.   They are theorists.

16.   They say, "You don't understand me!" This means, in other words, "You won't agree with me!"

17.   They often say, "God told me", thinking this will add weight to their argument.

18.   When corrected, they say, "I'll pray about it." To obey is better than_____ (1 Sam. 15:22; Prov. 19:16).

19.   They claim they have their own conscience, but of course this cannot apply where the government of the Church is concerned.

20.   The unteachable find it difficult to receive from people they know.

21.   They always hear for others, but not for themselves.

22.   They say they have heard it all before, never thinking that if it is being said again, then perhaps God is saying something to them.

23.   They are not responsive to prophecy. Their response is, "Oh! It's him again!"

24.   The unteachable do not have a submissive spirit towards authority.

25.   They get bored at meetings because, after all, they consider theirs to be THE important ministry!

Having just one or two of these symptoms does not necessarily mean he or she is unteachable as we all have attitudes and weaknesses. However, it does help us spot the unteachable when a number of these symptoms are continually manifested. It is wise regularly to_____ ourselves to see if we are still in the faith (2 Cor. 13:5; 1 Cor. 11:28).

Church is the greatest place on Earth when the people have good attitudes and allow themselves to be discipled in a scriptural manner. So let us be obedient. Let us not only be disciples ourselves, but go into all the world and make disciples of others, baptising them in the name of the Father, Son and Holy Spirit, and teaching them to obey everything Jesus commanded (Matt. 28:19-20).

CHAPTER 2
REPENTANCE

2. REPENTANCE

In Acts 2:38, Peter replied, "Repent and be baptised, every one of you, in the name of Jesus Christ for the forgiveness of your sins. And you will receive the gift of the Holy Spirit."

Repentance is found throughout the Bible. But why is there a need to repent?
(Mark 1:15, 6:12; Matt. 3:1-8, 4:17).

Rom. 10:10 says, "For it is with your heart that you believe and are justified and it is with your mouth that you confess and are saved."

WHY BELIEVE WITH YOUR HEART?

Jer. 17:9 says, "The heart is deceitful above all things and beyond cure. Who can understand it?"
In 2 Kings 8:7-15 Elisha stared at King-to-be Hazael and told him he would murder Israelites, kill children, set fire to homes and do evil things. In v13, Hazael asked how he could do such a thing – he did not see into his own heart - and yet Hazael went on to do all of these terrible things.
Hazael's heart was _____ about himself.
We all like to think we are better than we actually are.
We like to give the_____ that we are better than we actually are.

BELIEVING WITH THE HEART IS THE FIRST STEP TO REPENTANCE

'To repent' comes from *metanoeo*, a Greek word meaning 'to change your mind, thoughts or views'.

Repentance is not_____ of sin (Acts 2:37-38). They were cut to the heart, but they had not yet repented. They were just sorry.

Repentance is not_____. It is more than emotions.

Repentance is not_____ - "Sorry, I was found out."

Repentance is not a_____ to start again.

Repentance is not a_____ to just believe.

Is. 64:6 states that all our righteousness (goodness) is like dirty rags to a pure, holy, perfect God. The literal translation is that our best is like a menstrual cloth.

There are 103 defined sins in the Bible. So with that number, it is not surprising that in the New Testament, repentance is mentioned 60 times. Acts 17:30 commands us to repent.

REPENTANCE IS NECESSARY

Eph. 2:3 tells us we have an inborn desire to sin (to do wrong).
Rom. 3:23 tells us that, "All have sinned and fall short of the glory (standards) of God."

MEN OFTEN CHOOSE RELIGION TO EASE THEIR CONSCIENCE

For example, if you ask individuals the question as to whether they are a Christian, sample responses would be:

    A.   I am a Catholic, or I attend Church of England (or some other religious group);

    B.   I don't go to Church, but I am a good person (or I have not done bad things);

    C.   I believe in God;

    D.   I pray to God sometimes;

    E.   As long as I don't harm anybody, that's good enough.

Let's examine each comment from the Bible.

A.   The Pharisees were religious. There is no denomination or group that makes us Christian. 2 Tim. 3:5 talks about having a_____ of godliness, but without the power;

B.   Rom. 3:23 and 3:12 tell us that, "There is no-one_____, not even one" (in God's eyes);

C.   James 2:19 tells us, "Even the demons_____ - and shudder";

D.   Praying is speaking to God. But in Job 1:7, even Satan spoke to God;

E.   In 2 Kings 8:13, Hazael did not know the_____ in his own heart.

None of us is born a Christian, and so at some time in our life, we have to choose whether to repent or not with a 'yes' or a 'no'. 2 Cor. 6:2 says, "Now is the time of God's favour, now is the day of salvation."

HOW DO WE REPENT?

Rom. 10:10 teaches us that it is, "With your_____ that you confess." You need to:

A.   Acknowledge you cannot do it without Christ;

B.   Ask Jesus to forgive you;

C.   Receive your salvation (Rom. 10:13).

When real repentance has taken place, a genuine change takes place in our lives. There is_____ in Heaven (Luke 15:7).

To sum it up: unless true repentance takes place, we will have only a dead religion, or simply have no God in our lives. We cannot always have been a Christian and so there is a day and a time when we need to repent. It is a choice - a decision - that we make with a clear head: it is with the heart that we believe and with the mouth that we confess that Jesus Christ is our Lord and Saviour. Then the rest of our lives will be affected when we have a real, living relationship with Jesus.

CHAPTER 3
FAITH

3. FAITH

Rom. 14:23 says, "Everything that does not come from faith is sin."
Heb. 11:6 says, "Without faith it is impossible to please God."

In this lesson, we want to see a faith that is active, alive and effective, one that will take us to new levels of belief. In Eph. 1:18, Paul prays, "That the eyes of your heart may be enlightened in order that you might know the hope to which He has called you."

  A. Faith is the second principle of the doctrine of Christ (Heb. 6:1).

  B. Repentance and faith are tied together. They are_____ on each other (Mark 1:15; Acts 20:21).

Ern Baxter said, "To profess to turn to God without forsaking sin in repentance ends in hypocrisy, to attempt to forsake sin without turning to God in faith ends in failure and despair."

  C. Faith is the absolute foundation for the Christian life (Heb. 11:6). Without faith, it is_____ to please God.

The righteous_____ by faith (Rom. 1:17).

WHAT IS FAITH?

  A. Faith is believing for something that has not happened yet (Heb. 11:1).

  B. Charles Finney said, "Faith is an unqualified surrender of the will to God."

  C. When the Israelites sent spies to the Promised Land, how many were sent? We remember Joshua and Caleb, but not the rest, because nobody remembers faithless people.

D.   The Oxford Dictionary defines faith as 'complete trust or confidence, firm belief without logical proof'.

E.   The Greek word for faith is *pistis*, or 'firm persuasion'.

WHAT KIND OF FAITH?

There are various levels of faith that we stop at or grow into:

A.   Lack of faith (Greek *husterema*), meaning 'deficiency' or 'shortcoming' (1 Thess. 3:10).

B.   Weak faith (Greek *asthenes*), meaning 'strengthless' (Matt. 26:41).

C.   Little faith (Greek *micros*, the opposite of *megas*), meaning 'small' (Matt. 14:31, 16:8).

D.   Seed faith (Greek *sperno*), meaning 'to sow' (Matt. 17:20).

E.   Growing faith (Greek *auxano*), meaning 'to increase' (2 Cor. 10:15).

F.   Fast-growing faith (Greek *huperauxano*), or 'to increase beyond measure' (2 Thess. 1:3).

G.   Rich in faith (Greek *plousios*), or 'having plenty, abounding in, beyond the normal' (James 2:5).

H.   Strong faith (Greek *endinamono*), meaning 'to strengthen more' (Rom. 4:20).

I.   Great faith (Greek *tosoutos*), or 'so much of, quantity' (Luke 7:9; Matt. 15:21-28).

J.   Perfect faith (Greek *teleio*), meaning 'to finish, to complete, or to conclude' (James 2:22).

HOW DO WE GROW IN FAITH?

A.   The best source is the_____ to increase our faith (Rom. 10:17).

B.   Abraham is a good example as he:

Heard the Word;

Put his faith in the Word;

Refused anything that would contradict the Word;

Did not waver;

Saw the fulfilment of the Word (Heb. 11:8-12; Rom. 4:16-22).

C.   Faith is a condition of_____, not an act of the mind (Rom. 10:10).

HOW DO WE FUNCTION IN FAITH?

A. With the_____ (Rom. 10:9; Matt. 10:32). "Out of the overflow of the heart, the mouth speaks" (Matt. 12:34).

B. An act of_____ to the Word given. Faith and action are joined together (Rom. 1:5, 15:18, 16:26: James 2:14-26).

C. When trouble comes, do not complain because all of us have troubles. If we have no troubles, we do not need the faith. Musclemen build muscles by going through a pain barrier: no pain, no muscles. It is the same spiritually: we build spiritual muscles by the pain we go through (James 1:2-4). Jesus said, "In this world you will have trouble" (John 16:33).
Trouble builds faith.

WHAT IS THE DIFFERENCE BETWEEN AN OBSTACLE AND AN OPPORTUNITY?

It is our faith attitude towards it.

A. Rom. 8:28 says that God is working for our good. No matter how many promises God has made, they are yours in Christ (2 Cor. 1:20).

B. Accept the testing of your faith by being a doer of the Word (Heb. 6:12-15; Ps. 105:19). "(For) the testing of your faith develops perseverance. Perseverance must finish its work so that you may be mature and complete, not lacking anything" (James 1:3-4).

HOW TO INCREASE YOUR FAITH

A. Believe in your heart that God's Word is_____ (James 1:6; 2 Pet. 1:19).

B. Hear God's Word by_____ the Word (Rom. 10:17).

C. Hear the Word and_____ the Word. Do not be just a hearer (Luke 8:15).

D. Put into practice and_____ your faith (Matt. 9:20-21, 14:25-29).

E. _____ man's natural reasoning and philosophies that oppose God's Word (1 Tim. 1:4-7; 2 Tim. 2:16-18; Rom. 14:1; Col. 2:8).

CHAPTER 4
WATER BAPTISM

4. WATER BAPTISM

When we talk about baptism, it is important to allow the last word to be the Word of God, and not some religious opinion (Mark 7:8-9 and 13).

So what does the word 'baptise' symbolise? The word 'baptise' comes from a Greek word, *baptisma*, meaning 'the combined processes of immersion, submersion and emergence'. The Greek verb *baptizo* means 'to actively cause something or somebody to be fully submersed in water'. So water baptism is by_____ under the surface of water.

In Matt. 28:19, the verse should read, "Go and make disciples of all nations, immersing them in the name of the Father and of the Son and of the Holy Spirit."

WHY DO WE NEED TO BE BAPTISED?

Mark 16:16 tells us, "Whoever believes and is baptised will be saved, but whoever does not believe will be condemned." These are strong words, but strong because we are_____ to be baptised:

    A.   Jesus said, "If you love Me, you will obey what I command" (John 14:15).

    B.   The Apostles also commanded it (Acts 2:37-39, 10:44-48).

    C.   Jesus was the example (Matt. 3:13-17).

    D.   Obedience is the fruit of our service to Jesus and the Word (James 2:17).

Water baptism is not optional. Refusing water baptism is disobedience to God.

WHAT IS THE FOUNDATION FOR US TO BE BAPTISED?

A.   Acts 2:38 says, "_____ and be baptised."

B.   Acts 8:12 and Mark 16:16 advise us to_____ with understanding as this act is not for babies.

C.   When Jesus died, He was buried, but He did not stay buried. He rose again. When we are baptised, the Bible tells us that we are buried, but then arise like Jesus to a new life, leaving the past behind. So baptism_____ us with Jesus (Rom. 6:3-5). In Col. 2:12 and 3:1, we bury the old nature. In baptism, we crucify the old man and the new man arises to a_____ life.

D.   In the new life, we_____ sin (Rom. 6:11-18). Baptism_____ sin away (Acts 22:16). It is not the water that does it, but obedience to God allows the Holy Spirit to come into a clean life. 1 Cor. 10:2 speaks about Moses, saying that, "They (the Israelites) were all baptised...in the cloud and in the sea." Similarly, after they had passed through the Red Sea, it closed behind them, symbolising that the old life in Egypt was behind them and a new life lay ahead in the Promised Land. The same promise stands today for us in water baptism.

E.   Water baptism also deals with our sinful hearts (Col. 2:11-12).

In the Old Testament, God made an everlasting covenant with Abraham. Those partaking in this covenant were required to undergo natural circumcision of the flesh as a sign of their commitment to God's promise. In the New Testament, God has taken this natural ritual and replaced it with a spiritual requirement for all those who now belong to Christ (Gal. 3:29). In water baptism, we receive the spiritual experience of heart circumcision represented in the Old Testament by circumcision of the flesh. This natural ritual consisted of four elements that are all symbolic of something that now takes place in the circumcision of the heart (Rom. 2:29).

A.   In water baptism, we_____ the old sinful nature – we cut away flesh.

B.   In water baptism, it is a_____ to self – it is symbolic of the shedding of blood.

C.   In water baptism, it is a_____, a new life, a resurrected one (1 Pet. 3:20).

D.   In water baptism, we have a_____, the name of Jesus, the fulness of the Godhead bodily.

Jesus commanded that baptism was to be administered in the name of the Father and of the Son and of the Holy Ghost (Matt. 28:19-20). Later, after Jesus' ascension and exaltation (Acts 2:33-36), the disciples came to see that the name of the Son was that of the Lord Jesus Christ. When they baptised, they baptised in this manner (Acts 2:36-41, 8:12-16 and 35-38, 10:48).

How many times have we heard the saying, "I wish I could be baptised again as it was such a great experience?" Why? It is only water after all. The reason we say it, is because we have obeyed the Lord and so He blesses us.

If a man or a woman refuses baptism, then we have the right to question his or her walk with the Lord because the Bible does the same (1 Pet. 4:17). Judgement begins with the family of God.

If every believer was obedient to water baptism, it would open up a floodgate of blessing in the House of the Lord.

CHAPTER 5
HOLY SPIRIT BAPTISM

5. HOLY SPIRIT BAPTISM

Holy Spirit baptism is often thought of as the same experience as when we were first saved, but it is clear in the Bible that these are different works of the Holy Spirit. In John 20:22, Jesus breathed on the disciples with the Holy Spirit. However, in Acts 1:4-5, He said to the same disciples that they had to wait in Jerusalem as "in a few days you will be baptised with the Holy Spirit." So the baptism of the Holy Spirit is a different work to that of salvation.

WAS THE HOLY SPIRIT ACTIVE IN THE OLD TESTAMENT?

A. Bezalel was filled with the Spirit of God (Ex. 31:3), making him skilled in crafts. So the Holy Spirit enables men to do God-appointed tasks.

B. The Holy Spirit came upon Moses and his Elders (Num. 11:25).

C. In special times, the Holy Spirit was active in people's lives (Judg. 11:29). The Holy Spirit enabled Jephthah to destroy the Ammonites.

D. Othniel and Gideon both accomplished victory for the Lord when the Holy Spirit empowered them (Judg. 3:10-11, 6:34).

E. Samson did not have natural strength: it was only when the Holy Spirit came upon him that he was able to perform supernatural feats (Judg. 14:6).

In the Old Testament, the Holy Spirit came upon men and then withdrew (1 Sam. 10:6, 16:14). In John 1:33, John the Baptist said that the Messiah would come and the Holy Spirit would remain.

THE HOLY SPIRIT WAS ACTIVE IN CHRIST'S LIFE

Jesus Christ is our foundation and pattern for the flow of God through the Church.

CHRIST WAS	THE CHURCH IS TO BE
Born of the Spirit (Luke 1:35)	Born of the Spirit (John 3:5)
Filled with the Spirit (John 3:34)	Filled with the Spirit (Eph. 3:19)
Baptised with the Spirit (Matt. 3:16-17)	Baptised with the Spirit (Acts 1:5)
Led of the Spirit (Matt. 4:1)	Led of the Spirit (Rom. 8:14)
Sealed by the Spirit (John 6:27)	Sealed by the Spirit (Eph. 1:13)
Empowered by the Spirit (Luke 4:14)	Empowered by the Spirit (Acts 1:8)
Anointed by the Spirit (Acts 10:38)	Anointed by the Spirit (1 John 2:27)

IS THE HOLY SPIRIT HERE JUST TO HELP US?

A. In the modern Church, we regularly hear prayers that sound like this: "Come Holy Spirit, do a work, revive us, let us see miraculous signs and wonders, etc."

B. If I woke up in the morning and said, "Wife get my breakfast, clean up after that, vacuum the carpets, now I need some dinner, wash my car, get my supper, etc.", then what sort of a relationship would I have? A very poor one, and yet we use the Holy Spirit like this all the time.

2 Cor. 13:14 says, "The_____ of the Holy Spirit be with you all." This expression means 'an intimate relationship' with the third person of the Trinity. The Holy Spirit is a real person who can be_____ (Eph. 4:30).

As in a natural relationship where we learn intimacy, so the Holy Spirit longs to have an intimate relationship with God's people.

DO WE NEED TO BE BAPTISED IN THE HOLY SPIRIT?

A. Jesus was baptised in the Holy Spirit (Matt. 3:16; John 1:19-34). If Jesus who was perfect was baptised in the Spirit, how much more do we need to be?

B. Jesus baptised not with water, but with the Holy Spirit (John 1:33, 4:2).

C. Jesus promised life from within us, through the Holy Spirit (John 7:38-39).

D.   The Father, through Jesus, gave the Holy Spirit as promised (Acts 2:33).

WHY DOES GOD SEND THE HOLY SPIRIT?

A.   It was a_____ and a giving of_____
(Acts 1:4-5 and 8, 2:33 and 39; Luke 24:48).

B.   It is a separate_____ which we have or we don't have. Baptism in the Holy Spirit in the Early Church was classed as the foundation of our conversion (Acts 2:38).

WHAT HAPPENS WHEN WE ARE BAPTISED IN THE HOLY SPIRIT?

A.   All the people began to_____. Not some, but all the people (Acts 2:4).

B.   They declared the_____ of God.

C.   It was an experience which could be_____ (Acts 8:18 and 21).

D.   Cornelius and all the people_____ (Acts 10:44-46).

The Bible does not say 'tongues' is the evidence for Holy Spirit baptism, but wherever you read about people being filled with the Holy Spirit, you also read that they spoke in tongues.

CAN YOU BE A CHRISTIAN WITHOUT BEING BAPTISED IN THE HOLY SPIRIT?

A.   In Acts 19:1-6, Paul found some disciples who had been baptised in water, but had not heard about the Holy Spirit. So these Christians were_____ with the Holy Spirit. In verse 6, "Paul placed his hands on them and the_____ came on them and they_____ _____" when they found out there was such an experience.

B.   Being filled with the Holy Spirit gives Christians_____ to witness for Jesus to all men (Acts 1:8). We are much weaker when we have not received the power of the Holy Spirit.

C.   God desires everyone to be filled and to speak in tongues so that, when the tough times come, we have an instrument with which to_____ ourselves (1 Cor. 14:4).

D. Baptism in the Holy Spirit is for_____ who believe (Matt. 16:17; Acts 2:38-39).

WHY DOES GOD BAPTISE THE TONGUE?

A. The tongue causes most of our problems, so He baptised the tongue with_____ (Matt. 3:11).

B. Baptism and tongues is a_____ of the believer (Mark 16:17).

C. So we can worship the Lord (Acts 10:46).

D. So we can pray more effectively (Eph. 6:18).

HOW DO WE GET FILLED WITH THE HOLY SPIRIT?

A. We_____ Jesus to be filled with the Holy Spirit.

B. Thirst and hunger after righteousness (Matt. 5:6).

CHAPTER 6

THE LORDSHIP OF JESUS

6. THE LORDSHIP OF JESUS

Lordship means recognising God as sovereign.

Christ not only desires our salvation, but also that we would be true, committed and loyal followers of Him.

Jesus said to a crowd of people, "If anyone would come after Me, he must deny himself and take up his cross and follow Me. For whoever wants to save his life will lose it, but whoever loses his life for Me and for the Gospel will save it" (Mark 8:34-35).

A. Denying self means laying down MY will, MY desires, MY wants. Jesus prayed to His Father before His crucifixion, "Father, if You are willing, take this cup from Me; yet_____, but Yours be done" (Luke 22:42). Sometimes, we want to escape - from our families, our responsibilities, our circumstances – but God's will is to stay and accept the situation.

B. Suffering unjustly affects us as it affected Christ (1 Pet. 2:19-23, 3:13-18, 4:12-19).

C. We deny ourselves when we accept hardship (2 Tim. 2:3). We must also forgive those who offend us (Luke 23:34). There is no shame when we suffer for the Lord (Is. 50:7). Jesus, with joy at the things set before Him, endured the cross (Heb. 12:2).

D. Jesus entrusted His life to God (Luke 23:46). He gave His life into God's_____. If you do not deny yourself, then you will begin to feel sorry for yourself. In Matt. 16:22-23, when Jesus spoke about His death, Peter exclaimed, "Never Lord! This shall never happen to You!" You can translate this as 'have pity on yourself'. Jesus replied to Peter, "Get behind Me, Satan! You are a stumbling block to Me!" Pity is not in the mind of God, but in the minds of men. If

Satan succeeds in convincing us to feel sorry for ourselves, he paralyses our faith. So the Lordship of Christ in our lives is to reject_____ (Lam. 3:39).

E. Self-pity makes us live without a godly faith. Ten spies went into Canaan, the land God had promised. They saw giants, the Nephilim, descendants of Anak. The spies reported, "We seemed like grasshoppers in our_____ " (Num. 13:33). Circumstances without the Lordship of Christ appear as giants. When David faced Goliath, he said, "The battle_____ " (1 Sam. 17:47). "The Lord is with me like a mighty warrior" (Jer. 20:11).

F. To follow Jesus means He is our_____ (Matt. 10:24).

G. It means we are willing to be_____ and instructed in His ways.

H. It means we are willing to_____ to His commands (Luke 6:46; Matt. 7:21).

I. It means that we are willing to be_____ and adjusted by the Word (Prov. 3:11-12; Heb. 12:5-13).

TO DENY OURSELVES MEANS EVERYTHING IS SECONDARY TO THE LORD

A. Our_____ (Matt. 8:20; Luke 9:58).

B. Our_____ and relatives (Matt. 10:37-38).

C. Our_____ (Matt. 4:18-22).

D. Our_____ (Matt. 19:16-22).

The Lord demands nothing, but looks for willing hearts and minds, to offer these up if He asks (Matt. 16:24-26).

The Lord never asks us to give something up unless He plans to give us something in return (Mark 10:29-30; John 10:10).

Denying ourselves has a purpose to it:

A. So we become_____ Christians, able to handle the storms of life (Eph. 4:13-14).

B. To_____ Christ to the world (Eph. 4:13; Acts 11:26).

C. To be the kind of Christian for_____, being the example for their lives (1 Cor. 11:1; Titus 2:7-8).

D. To be the kind of Christian God can use to_____ to others (John 15:8, 12:7).

E. So that on the Day of Judgement the Lord will say "_____, good and faithful servant" (Matt. 25:21).

"If you do these things, you will never fall" (2 Pet. 1:10-11).

Living at the level God intends is a life of surrender to Him (Rom. 12:1-2).

> ## LORD OF ALL, OR NOT LORD AT ALL

CHAPTER 7
FELLOWSHIP

7. FELLOWSHIP

God never intended us to live in isolation, but for us to have good relationships with each other, flowing together as one to touch the world.

Eph. 4:1-6 talks about being patient and bearing with one another in love, whilst keeping the spirit of unity and peace.

WHAT DOES LIVING IN HARMONY MEAN?

If you listen to a great classical pianist, it really is a pleasant sound. However, if you listen to a novice who hits all the wrong notes, it is jarring to the ears. That is called disharmony. Disharmony in the Church is jarring to our spirit, but harmony in the Church is pleasant to our spirit.

WHAT IS FELLOWSHIP?

Fellowship in Greek is *koynonia*, meaning 'having a thing in common, to share or walk together'.

    A.   To the people of God, fellowship is_____ with each other, or a relationship we enter into by salvation and mutual participation in the Body.

    B.   Fellowship is in_____, both vertical and horizontal. When we fellowship, it is with each other, but it is also with the Father and the Son along with the Holy Ghost (1 John 1:3; 2 Cor. 13:14).

    C.   Vertical fellowship is_____, which is the cement for all other fellowship as we allow God's authority in our lives and lay down our own wills (1 Cor. 1:9; Eph. 2:12-18). When we are out of sync with the Lord, we are out of sync with each other.

D.   Horizontal fellowship is_____, with each other. Fellowship with the Lord establishes fellowship with each other through inter-relating (Acts 2:42). Pubs, clubs and other venues try to copy this, but in reality are poor substitutes.

Fellowship is experienced in many ways.

Practical Ways	Spiritual Ways
Receiving one another into friendship (Rom. 15:7)	Praying one for another (James 5:16)
Serving one another in practical ways (Gal. 5:13)	Exhorting one another (Heb. 3:13, 10:25)
House-to-house fellowship (Acts 2:46)	Edifying one another (Rom. 14:19)
Showing hospitality to those in need (Rom. 12:13)	Bearing one another's burdens (Gal. 6:2)
Being considerate, one to another (Eph. 4:32)	Singing, praising and worshipping together (Col. 3:16)
Helping the needy financially (1 John 3:16-18)	Comforting one another (1 Thess. 4:18)
Getting to know and appreciate each other (Acts 2:42-47)	Forgiving one another (Eph. 4:32)

Jesus gave a new commandment, to love each other. Why? So that, "By this all_____ that you are my disciples, if you love one another" (John 13:34-35). Satan constantly undermines fellowship by placing offences in the way.

HOW DO WE HANDLE OFFENCES?

A.   "If your brother sins against you, go and show him his fault, just between _____ of you" (Matt. 18:15).

B.   If we follow the Lord's instructions, offences rarely go beyond this command. Then the only time others are called upon is in extreme cases where the Elders of the Church may get involved. This procedure really does keep harmony and peace in the Church.

WHEN IS FELLOWSHIP UNWISE?

Doing things with our old friends as we did before we were Christians is unwise (2 Cor. 6:14 and 17). Paul wrote this to the Corinthian Church because he saw the negative effect it was having on Christians.

James 3:11 asks, "Can salt water and fresh water flow from the same spring?" No, that is impossible. We can no longer do what the world does and live a Christian lifestyle.

Nor must we have any fellowship with false religions. The whole of 2 Pet. 2 talks about false teachers, while Jude 4 says that fellowship is unwise with godless men who change the grace of our God into a licence for immorality. God has placed on us limitations, with others who profess Christianity, but who do not have the lifestyle.

Avoid:

A. _____ that undermines basic salvation or attacks the deity of Christ and the virgin birth, or that disagrees with the death and resurrection of Christ, the depravity of man outside of Christ, or the power of the blood of Jesus to clean men from all sins (Titus 3:10; Rom. 6:17). Unity can never be at the expense of truth.

B. Fellowship with those having_____that bring reproach on the Lord's name (Matt. 18:15-17; 1 John 1:7, 2:10-11; 2 Thess. 3:6): those who are greedy, abusive, or drunken, who use bad language or indulge in illicit sex and all who refuse to reconcile an offence with a brother or sister. They are like an umbilical cord which once gave life, but after the birth of the new baby, needs cutting off lest poisons feed back into the new baby.

We are not to_____ with them or_____ with them (1 Cor. 5:11; 2 Thess. 3:14). God is building His Church and one day it will be without spot or blemish. The Lord seeks that we all accept each other and are united to do His work for the Lord's family on Earth.

Chapter 8
PRIDE

8. PRIDE

THE PROBLEM WITH PRIDE

Prov. 16:16-20 says, "Pride goes before destruction". We all wrestle with_____.

Pride is the difference between joy and sadness, and pride does more to ruin homes and nations than any other sin.

Pride is a deceitful sin. Hell is filled with the sin of pride more than with any other sin. A drunk knows he is a drunk, but proud people seldom recognise when they are filled with pride. Though Jesus came from an eternal realm where God exalted Him to the highest place (Phil. 2:9-11), we see in John 13 and in Phil. 2:6-8 that He humbled Himself. Jesus tried to wash Simon Peter's feet, but he would not allow Him to do so at first. So Jesus told him, "Unless I wash you, you will have no part of Me." At this, Simon Peter asked Him to wash him all over. Pride stopped Peter's feet being washed, while his response was not humble.

Rom. 12:3 describes how pride is not a good assessment of self.

The main problem in Church comes from Bible-carrying Christians who believe they have gifting. In Acts 8:33, Jesus was deprived of justice, but He did not reject the world because He was hurt. When we claim to be hurt, it comes from pride – from what has been done to me. Pride can ruin your life and affect your future.

WHAT IS PRIDE?

A.   Pride is an attitude of independence from God – "I can handle things by myself." When we don't pray, it is not prayerlessness that is the problem, but it is us feeling we don't need to pray, believing we can handle the situation ourselves.

B.   Pride is the spirit of ungratefulness towards God – God gave us everything we have – our ingenuity, our strength and our energy.

C.   Pride means we esteem ourselves better than others. "Pride goes before destruction" (Prov. 16:18).

How do we see this working out in people's lives?

A.   Proud people get irritated when corrected (Prov. 12:1).

B.   The proud accept praise for things out of their control – when the Lord blesses, the proud think it is their ability.

C.   Pride does not admit to mistakes – but will blame-shift.

D.   Pride in a dispute says, "I can get along without you." So we don't speak, or we leave the relationship or Church.

E.   Pride refuses advice from other people. "He who scorns instruction will_____ for it" (Prov. 13:13).

F.   Pride often shows itself in competition with others – C.S. Lewis said, "Pride often gets no pleasure out of having something, but only out of having more of it than another man. We say that people are proud of being rich or clever or good-looking, but they are not. They are proud of being richer, cleverer or better-looking. It is the comparison that makes us proud, the pleasure of being above others."

FOUR WAYS PRIDE WILL RUIN AND DEVASTATE YOUR LIFE

1. Pride Defies God and He_____ pride (Prov. 6:16-19).

A.   Why does God hate pride so much? Lucifer was established in pride. He was the Son of the Morning and became the Father of Night. In 1 Tim. 3:6, Paul gave us the standard of a Leader so we do not fall into_____ and come under the same judgement as the Devil.

B.   Pride_____ the human race and brought sin into the world. "As long as you are proud, you cannot know God" (C.S. Lewis). A man who is proud is always looking down on things and people – as long as you are looking down, you cannot see anything above you.

C. "God opposes the proud but gives grace to the humble" (1 Pet. 5:5; James 4:6). The Greek word for 'oppose' is *antikeimai*, meaning 'sets against', 'resists' or 'is hostile to'.

D. Pride will destroy your life. All heartache, tears, wars, pain, shame, conflict are the outcome of pride. It wrecked the human race.

2. Pride defiles man

A. Prov. 16:5 says, "_____of this: (the proud) will not go unpunished." Prov. 21:4 states that the proud heart is a wicked sin.

B. Where does pride come from? We are born with pride – it comes out of the heart (Mark 7:21-22; Prov. 21:4). A worm will burrow out of an apple, and not into it, because the eggs are laid on the apple blossom and hatch inside the fruit. Prov. 14:12 tells us that what seems right to us, in the end leads to death.

C. Seeking signs is often out of pride. Matt. 12:39 warns us that a wicked generation asks for signs. The Corinthian Church mistook_____for God's approval.

D. Claiming Satan is attacking us is often out of pride and conceit, especially when we never win souls or we are ineffective. Each day has its own trouble (Matt. 6:34, 5:45). Most trouble in life is NOT Satan attacking us directly. It is often:
The circumstances of life (economic downturn, joblessness, pollution, inflation, accidents);
The consequences of the flesh which are simply _____.
Sow to the flesh, you reap things of the flesh – sow to the Spirit and you will reap things of the Spirit (Gal. 6:8).

3. Pride in managing your own life

A. Hag.1:6 states living like this is like having 'a purse with holes in it'. It is giving nothing or little to God because we do not trust Him – "I will manage my own finances".

B. Mal. 3:8-9 talks about placing_____ 'under a curse' because we rob God. So we can have either blessing and protection, or exposure and a curse. God does not need your money, but if He does not have your money, He does not have your_____ (Matt. 6:21).

4. **Pride of knowledge**

   A. Knowledge puffs up, it makes arrogant (1 Cor. 8:1).

   B. A way seems right to us, but the end leads to death (Prov. 14:12).

   C. Each perspective is right: that's the reason married couples never stop having conflict. Often, we don't want a relational problem to be solved, we just want_____ the argument (James 4:1).

   D. "God opposes the proud" (James 4:6), but "humble yourselves.... and He (God) will lift you up"'(James 4:10).

CONCLUSION

God hates the proud, but will bless, exalt and lift up the humble. He wants a Church where the individuals are not self-seeking, but where the Lord has their full attention and all their hearts as in Matt. 22:37 where it says, "Love the Lord your God with all your heart". Then there is release of blessing, joy and life, not only for the individual, but for the whole Church.

CHAPTER 9
HOLINESS

9. HOLINESS

Over many years in the Western World, in what we call Church, there has been a paradigm shift from integrity and holiness to a gross imitation of worldly behaviour by trying to be relevant. This has led to many Leaders building Church without a biblical framework. As a result, there are those who claim to be Christians, but who do not have surrendered lives.

A type of language that is often not wholesome is spoken from the pulpit. 1 Pet. 4:11 says that when we speak, we should speak 'the very words of God'.

WHAT IS HOLINESS?

Holiness in Greek is *hagiasmos*, meaning 'set apart for sacred use'. In 1 Pet. 1: 13-16, we are given a definition of what holiness is and encouraged to be holy. We are not to 'conform to the evil desires (we) had when (we) lived in ignorance', but to 'be holy in all (we) do'.

Where there is no_____, people cast off restraint (Prov. 29:18).

WHAT IS REVELATION?

Paul said that, "The mystery (was) made known to me by revelation" (Eph. 3:3).

A. A communication of the knowledge of God to the soul, or an expression of the mind of God for instruction to the Church. Some Churches draw in numbers of people by casting off restraint: you could easily be in a nightclub with the same kind of atmosphere. CHURCH CAN BE BUILT WITHOUT GOD.

B.   Many times people ask, "What is God's will?" 1 Thess. 4:3 answers that question: "It is God's will that you should be sanctified." If a conference is organised for signs and miracles, or for the prophetic, it will be full, but if a conference is organised for holiness, then few will attend.

C.   We do not live like society or the world because we have been_____ from the nations to be God's own.

D.   We are distinctly different – a different DNA – a different sound – a different call.

WHY HOLINESS?

A.   No man will see the Lord without holiness (Heb. 12:14).

B.   We cannot offer the same in God's House as the world offers.

C.   Holiness leads to eternal life (Rom. 6:22). This indicates that without holiness we will not have eternal life.

D.   When Israel came out of Egypt, Egypt was not out of them. Often, those who claim to be Christian come out of the world, but the world is not out of them.

HOW DO WE AFFECT THE WORLD?

A.   Follow the decrees of the Lord and the nations will hear about it and say that these are wise and understanding people (Deut. 4:5-6).

B.   We are the treasured possession, and if we keep His commands, He will set us above the nations and we will be holy to the Lord (Deut. 26:18-19).

HAGIASMOS OR HOLINESS CHANGES US

A.   *Hagiasmos* sees other people as holy and so we don't bad-mouth them (1 Pet. 3:10).

B.   *Hagiasmos* gives power to the Church (Acts 2:40-47).

C.   *Hagiasmos* does not compromise with evil: today, when adultery is committed, we hear that someone has 'fallen'. In fact, that person has been exposed.

The Bible talks about holiness from Genesis to Revelation:
Holy God, Holy Father, Holy Spirit, Holy nations, Holy people, Holy temple, Holy law, Holy name, Holy angels, Holy hands, Holy calling, Holy women, Holy hill, Holy day, Holy kiss.

WHY DOES GOD WANT A HOLY PEOPLE?

A. For_____ (Acts 15:14).

B. To purify a people for_____, eager to do what is right.

C. To have a holy nation, a people_____ to God. Christ gave Himself up for the Church, to present her without stain or blemish, but_____ and blameless (Eph. 5:25-27). The wisdom of the world is_____ (1 Cor. 3:19). So why do we copy it?

D. To purify for Himself a people whose responsibility is to purify themselves (2 Cor. 7:1; 1 Sam. 16:5; 2 Tim. 2:21; Lev. 11:44, 20:7-8; Rev. 19:7).

E. We have a responsibility to discipline our lives and to have a separate, clean life (Deut. 7:2-3 and 6).

HOW CAN WE HAVE *HAGIASMOS*, AND BE SEPARATE, DIFFERENT AND UNIQUE?

The answer is:

A. To control the 'one-eyed creature' in most of our lives – the computer. Master what we see. There are companies with programs which protect us from stumbling onto unwholesome sites.

B. To master the television, especially as children receive their value system from it.

I am not saying to throw them out, but master the mouse or controls.

HOW DO WE PUT *HAGIASMOS* INTO THE YOUTH?

Young people allow feelings to dictate their lives. As feelings are frequently mistaken for love, young people can then marry purely because of feelings, and find themselves in a loveless marriage when those feelings wear off. A high percentage of Church kids admitted to having had sex outside of marriage, and those are just the ones who were honest.

A. Not only is marrying an unbeliever unwise, but we can also be unequally yoked to another believer (2 Cor. 6:14).

B. Men have a big responsibility. In Gen. 3, Eve was tempted and she took the forbidden fruit, but it was to the man that God came (Gen. 3:9), to call him to account.

C.   A man called Naboth had a vineyard and King Ahab desired it. So his wife Jezebel, decided to get it for him (1 Kings 21:7). She used the King's seal on letters to arrange for Naboth's death, after which she told Ahab to go and take possession of the vineyard. Jezebel wrote the letter, planned, schemed and manipulated, but God came to the man   (1 Kings 21:17-18).

D.   The seed of headship is on the man (Gen. 3:16; 1 Pet. 3:1). But like Adam, men can often abdicate their responsibility to teach holiness to the young, and instead leave it to their wives or Sunday School teachers.

E.   Teach the children so the understanding of the seed of headship is transferred to them (Deut. 6:6-9, 4:9, 11:18-19).

F.   The Bible talks about holy women (Phil. 4:2; Acts 16:14). This world would seem to pressurise women into having a certain look, height or weight, when in fact women were created with larger bodies in order to bear children. It is not a sin to look bigger: it is normal. Looking beautiful does not come from what modern so-called experts say women should look like. Holy women have an inner beauty that shines through the outer (1 Pet. 3:2-5).

THE BIBLE ASKS US TO BE DIFFERENT AND TO HAVE A DIFFERENT CULTURE

In Gen. 18:19, Abraham_____ to direct his children so the Lord could do what He promised.

A.   When your son asks about laws and stipulations, you can_____ (Deut. 6:20-21).

B.   Be holy in all that you do because the_____ stands forever (1 Pet. 1:13-25).

C.   How do the young stay pure? By living_____to the Word. We cannot take what the world offers and give it back to the world.

D.   We do not belong to the world (John 15:19). Holiness on Earth prepares us for Heaven (Rev. 21:27).

E.   _____ comes out of holiness (Heb. 1:9). Happy Churches are holy Churches.

Religion has brought weirdness into God's house. <u>The Lord is seeking a people who are distinctly different from the world and are not a copy of it.</u> Holiness does not make us odd, but brings normality into our lives. Without holiness, we are simply religious.

WITHOUT HOLINESS, NO MAN WILL SEE GOD (Heb. 12:14)

CHAPTER 10
COMMUNION

10. COMMUNION

1 Cor. 11:23-26 refers to Jesus when He broke the bread and said to His disciples, "This is My body which is broken for you; do this in remembrance of Me." He then sipped the wine and said, "This cup is the new covenant in My blood; do this, whenever you drink it, in remembrance of Me." We continue to do this because we proclaim the Lord's death until He comes again.

There are many names given to the breaking of bread. Some are from the Bible and some are historical or traditional:

A.   The Lord's Supper is so-called because Jesus had a supper with the disciples prior to His crucifixion (Matt. 26:26-29). This scripture was a prophetic statement which pointed to a time when believers would again eat a supper with Jesus. This event is called the_____ of the Lamb (Rev. 19:9 and 17).

B.   The Lord's_____ reminds us of a great feast where there is love and fellowship, a place where we are invited to enjoy an intimacy with the Lord.

C.   The_____ speaks of intimacy and sharing, both with each other and with the Lord Jesus Christ (1 Cor. 10:16).

D.   The Breaking of_____ refers to the time when Jesus broke the bread with His disciples and then blessed it (Acts 20:7; Matt. 26:26).

E.   Some new biblical names include: The Eucharist (from the Greek word *eucharistia* meaning 'giving thanks'); The Sacrament (from a Latin word meaning 'holy' or 'set apart').

HOW ARE WE TO PARTICIPATE?

A.   Churches and denominations often break bread in a quiet atmosphere, with either the priest or Church officers walking around, giving the bread and wine to each person. But how did Jesus do it? In Luke 22:14, it says, "Jesus and His Apostles_____ at the table."

So it was a very relaxed time. John 13:23 says, "The one Jesus loved reclined next to Him." The table was not of a western type, but it was about knee-high and individuals would sit on a cushion on the floor, with the right elbow on the table. This was typical of the Passover meal during the Roman period. The table was called a triclinium.

B. Jesus "took bread, gave thanks and_____, and gave it to them" (Luke 22:19). It was not in little squares, but a good chunk of bread to share with each other. So we can see the picture, the disciples breaking bread and praying with each other and giving thanks to God.

C. "In the same way....He took the cup" (Luke 22:20). Communion is not meant to be sombre, but to be a celebration as we remember what Jesus has done for us (Matt. 26:17-30; Mark 14:12-26; Luke 22:17-20).

HOW DID JESUS ESTABLISH COMMUNION?

A. By using bread (Luke 22:19). Bread represented the_____ of Christ which was broken for sinful men and women. Jesus said of the bread that it was necessary for spiritual life (John 6:58).

B. In Matt. 26:29, Jesus spoke about the fruit of the_____ which represents the _____ of Christ Jesus that was poured out for sinful men. The blood of Christ was poured out in seven ways:

   1. He sweated blood in the garden (Luke 22:44);

   2. His face was beaten, which was the second sprinkling (Matt. 26:67);

   3. He was flogged with whips and His flesh was torn open (Matt. 27:26; Is.50:6);

   4. They pulled out His beard (Is 50:6) and He lost the appearance of a man;

   5. They placed on His head a crown of thorns (Matt. 27:29-30);

   6. He was crucified with nails through His hands and feet (Ps. 22:16; Rev. 1:7);

   7. His blood was poured out when they pierced His side (John 19:34).

So when we have communion and remember His broken body, and then take the cup representing His blood, it emphasises the power that the blood of Christ has. Heb. 12:24 says that the blood of Christ "speaks a better word than the blood of Abel". For this blood cleanses from all sin (1 John 1:7).

C. Because of the supernatural power of the blood and the bread representing the Body of Christ, scripture tells us that before we participate in communion, we should_____ ourselves to make sure we are free from any offence towards man or God (Luke 22:21; 1 Cor. 11:28-29). Otherwise, it could just become a formality during which we would have no intimacy with the Lord.

D.   Communion is a time to_____the death and resurrection of Jesus and_____ all the things Christ has done for us.

E.   We are to be_____ because we are all partakers of one loaf (1 Cor. 10:17).

F.   Communion is a time of_____ our relationships, which can bring physical healing to our bodies (1 Cor. 11:29-30). It is possible to break bread and have a wrong relationship with another member. Quite often, this is the reason why some people have illnesses in their lives.

G.   It is a time of celebration, giving_____ to the Lord (Matt. 26:27).

H.   To fully appreciate and understand communion and prevent it from becoming mere ritual, we need to ask the Lord to give us a_____ concerning the Lord's Table. Paul the Apostle loved the Table of the Lord because he had an incredible revelation about it himself (1 Cor. 11:23).

I.   We cannot have an offence against anyone in the Body of Christ and go on to break bread and drink from the cup, because it has serious consequences. It is vital that we have right relationships with each other. Matt. 5:23-24 cautions us: "If you are offering your gift at the altar and there remember that your brother has something against you, leave your gift there in front of the altar. First go and be reconciled to your brother; then come and offer your gift."

J.   If we follow biblical guidelines as in Matt. 18:15-17, all relationships in the House of the Lord can be sweet.

K.   If we have an offence, we should not speak about it to anyone else. The biblical principle is that we speak to the person concerned and keep it just between the two of us (Matt. 18:15). This principle succeeds almost every time and can bring reconciliation to relationships.

Communion is an incredible time when we are put in right relationship with the Lord and with each other. The heart of the Lord is to bless His people through the bread and the cup of blessing.

Chapter 11

KINGDOM STEWARDSHIP

11. KINGDOM STEWARDSHIP

DEFINITION OF CHRISTIAN STEWARDSHIP

Christian stewardship is the practice of understanding that our time, abilities and material possessions are given to us by God (James 1:17). It is based on the conviction that He trusts us to use these gifts primarily to serve His Church and benefit His Kingdom to the best of our ability. It is a divine/human partnership, with God as the Senior Partner.

For what purpose have we been given talents, abilities and time? 1 Cor. 6:19-20 tells us that our bodies belong to God, that they are not our own but have been bought at a price, and that we need to honour God with our bodies.

HOW DO WE HONOUR GOD WITH OUR BODIES?

In Luke 16:1-2, there was a rich man whose manager was accused of wasting his possessions. So he called him in and asked him to give an account of his management.

A. Stewardship is_____ our lives. How we manage our time and life can honour or dishonour God.

B. In the New Testament culture, as now, rulers and wealthy people gave delegated authority to stewards to oversee the servants or slaves and property of the owner.

C. God is the owner of everything (Gen. 14:19; Ps. 24:1, 50:1-12; Hag. 2:8).

D. We give an account to God for the stewardship He has given us (Rom. 14:12).

E. God gives rewards to those who seek Him (Heb. 11:6).

F. In Matt. 25:14-30, there is an example of faithful stewards and lazy stewards. One steward doubled what he was given and was called 'good and faithful'. The one who did nothing with what he was given was called 'wicked and lazy'. He was busy doing nothing with what he had been given.

G. All our talents and abilities have been given to us ultimately for the Lord's Church. "What do you have that you did not receive? And if you did receive it, why do you boast as though you did not?" (1 Cor. 4:7).

WHAT DOES KINGDOM STEWARDSHIP INVOLVE?

A. It involves us giving our_____ (1 Cor. 6:19; Rom. 12:1; Acts 17:25).

B. It is an honourable use of our_____
(Ps. 90:12; Prov. 24:30-34).

C. It is a giving of our_____ (Matt. 25:14-30).

D. It is an understanding of correctly using our_____
(Matt. 6:19-21; Col. 3:1-2).

E. Wise stewardship is a thoughtful and purposeful use of all
our_____ (1 Cor. 16:1-2).

WHAT IS THE FOUNDATION OF A GOOD STEWARD?

A. He has a servant's spirit: he will do whatever task he is given (Matt. 23:11-12).

B. He is not proud, but_____ (1 Pet. 5:5).

C. He is faithful and loyal (1 Cor. 4:1-2; Matt. 21:38-41).

D. He is zealous (Rom. 12:11) and passionate about what he does.

JESUS TAUGHT THE PRINCIPLE OF STEWARDSHIP

We see teaching on stewardship in Luke 16:1-13 and in Matt. 25:14-30.

A. If we do not use what God has given us, we will_____.

B. We are to bring_____ to the Kingdom.

WHO IS GREAT IN THE KINGDOM?

A. Many ministries and functions love to have titles, such as 'Apostle' or 'Prophet'. Some like to be called 'Pastor' or 'Teacher' or 'Evangelist' but according to scripture, none of these giftings was meant to be used as a title (Matt. 23:8-10).

B. The greatest among you will be called your_____ (Matt. 23:7-10).

C. "Everyone who_____ himself will be humbled, and he

who_____ himself will be exalted" (Luke 14:11).

D. Jesus who was God made Himself_____, taking the nature of a

_____ (Phil. 2:7).

E. Therefore, God_____ Him to the highest place.

F. Those who use the talents and gifts they are given to build the House of the Lord.

Gifts are not given to make us look good, but to give back to God to use as He

wants.

G. Do I use my talents, time, abilities and finances to bring glory to God?

H. Do I give my talents to extend the Kingdom of God?

I. Do I steward my life in such a manner that God will say, "Well done, good and

faithful servant!"?

J. The greatest in the Kingdom are those who use their time and talents to serve the

Church and people to build His House (1 Pet. 4:10).

We belong to God: we are not our own for we are bought at a price. "Therefore honour

God with your body" (1 Cor. 6:19-20) and in your spirit, both of which are God's.

CHAPTER 12
A PEOPLE IN COVENANT

12. A PEOPLE IN COVENANT

Covenant is a topic not fully understood in this modern generation. So we are going to look at scripture to give us an understanding of this amazing part of God's plan on behalf of Himself, the Church and His people.

In the book of Exodus, Moses led a people called Israel out of Egypt. All the things that happened to Israel "were written down as warnings for us, on whom the fulfilment of the ages has come" (1 Cor. 10:11).

SO WHAT CHARACTERISTICS WAS GOD LOOKING FOR IN THESE ISRAELITES?

A. What God was looking for was a_____ for Himself (Acts 15:14; Titus 2:14; 1 Pet. 2:9-10). The Concise Oxford English Dictionary describes a people as 'a nation, right thinking people, having an identity, recognising ancestors, having roots and a history, fathers and patriarchs'.

B. God is looking for an emphasis on this definition of 'A PEOPLE' in every part of Church, stressing the idea of a patriarch (a father, fathers of the human race), patrimony (an inheritance from an ancestor), a common identity handed down to children.

C. Without an identity, we have no roots.

D. Our Father God filled the Earth with people because He loves people.

E. From Abraham came a people. God made a covenant with them, saying, "I will be their God, and they will be My people" (Heb. 8:10).

F. God had only one denomination called the children of_____ (Gal. 3:7).

The disciples saw miracles, healings, the raising of the dead and the casting out of demons, but the hardest thing for the disciples to do was to live together as a covenant people.

JESUS SAID, "GO AND MAKE DISCIPLES" (MATT. 28:19)

What Jesus meant was that we are to go and pass on our patrimony and identity as a people.

A.   "Once you WERE NOT a people, but now you_____ the people of God" (1 Pet. 2:10).

B.   God said, "Let us make man in our image, in our likeness" (Gen. 1:26): this means 'in our togetherness, not alone, in harmony like us, Father, Son and Holy Spirit'. We are to pass on what we are.

HEBREW FOR COVENANT IS TRANSLATED AS 'TO CUT A COVENANT'

A.   A covenant was made by sacrifice (Gen. 15:7-21; Ps. 50:5). An animal was cut in half; men would walk in the trail of blood and make a covenant with each other, saying, "My life and all I have is yours. If anyone attacks you, they attack me also."

B.   The New Testament is called the new covenant and confirms the old. God established a covenant with Abraham and said, "Kings will come from you" (Gen. 17:6).

David and Jonathan made a covenant (1 Sam. 18:3).

HOW DID DAVID AND JONATHAN MAKE A COVENANT?

A.   They stood in the_____ of the animal and made a covenant (1 Sam. 18:3).

B.   Jonathan gave David his tunic, sword, belt and bow, signifying "all I have is yours" (1 Sam. 18:4).

C.   They learned to cry with each other – such is the intimacy of covenant (1 Sam. 20:41).

D.   David and Jonathan loved each other (1 Sam. 18:3; 2 Sam. 1:26).

E.   They became_____ in spirit (1 Sam. 18:1).

WHAT EFFECTS DOES COVENANT HAVE?

A.   Covenant has long term effects: David cared for Mephibosheth because Jonathan was his father (2 Sam. 9:7).

B.   Melchizedek, King of Salem,_____ Abram and brought bread and wine (Gen. 14:18-20). Bread and wine is a covenant meal.

C.   No_____ word should come from our mouths because we give an_____ (Matt. 12:36). So in effect, covenant tames the tongue.

D.   In covenant, we_____ blessings and_____ blessings. Melchizedek blessed Abram in the name of the Creator of Heaven and Earth. The word creator here in Hebrew means 'the possessor of Heaven and Earth'.

E.   God possesses the Earth and everything in it. His plan is to bring Heaven to Earth as in the prayer of Jesus: let "Your will be done on Earth as it is in Heaven" (Matt. 6:10). God's plan for the Earth is a_____ of people walking in covenant as one nation.

GOD'S PLAN HAS NEVER CHANGED

A.   Everything may change but God remains the same (Heb. 1:10-12, 13:8; James 1:17).

B.   If we keep the covenant we will be blessed (Deut. 28:1-14).

C.   If we abuse covenant, we can become sick and put ourselves under a curse (Deut. 28:15-68; 1 Cor. 11:30). Some do break covenant, as Adam did (Hosea 6:7).

WE CANNOT BE FULFILLED WITHOUT GOD'S PLAN FOR COVENANT

God is a covenant God, marriage is covenant, family and friendships are covenant. God is building His Church and the plan He has for a people walking in covenant still stands true today through the blood poured out on the cross. So you can choose to walk in covenant or you can refuse, but it is only a covenant people who will see the dynamics of Heaven open up.

CHAPTER 13
FAITH & FINANCES

13. FAITH & FINANCES

Teaching on finances can have more of an effect on individuals than any other subject. The Bible teaches that every believer is accountable to God in the area of their personal finances. Our response and attitude to this matter can be a blessing or a curse in our lives.

"Whoever sows sparingly will also reap sparingly, and whoever sows generously will also reap generously. Each man should give what he has decided in his heart to give, not reluctantly or under compulsion, for God loves a cheerful giver. And God is able to make all grace abound to you, so that in all things at all times, having all that you need, you will abound in every good work" (2 Cor. 9:6-8).

IS IT IN ORDER TO TALK ABOUT MONEY?

A. Yes, as one in every six verses in the New Testament makes a reference to money.

B. The Gospels give warnings concerning the misuse of money more than any other single subject, while one in every four verses in Matthew, Mark and Luke deals with money.

C. In the Early Church, one of the first sins was the misuse of money (Acts 5:1-10).

THE HOUSE OF THE LORD WOULD NOT FUNCTION WITHOUT MONEY

Some of the things money is needed for include: staff salaries, heating, lighting, chairs, Sunday School materials, carpets, printed material, spreading the Gospel, full-time Elders, taxes, sundry materials and bills, photocopying, computers, printers.

SO HOW DOES THE LORD SUPPLY THE NEED?

Through the tithe:

A.   Tithe is a Hebrew word meaning a_____ or ten percent. It means systematically giving ten percent of our income back to the Lord for His work.

B.   Tithing was never a part of the_____, as men used to give to God prior to the giving of the Law (Gen. 14:18-20, 28:22).

C.   When the Law was given, the tithe was already part of the Lord's financial system (Lev. 27:30-33; Num. 18:20-32).

D.   Jesus also confirmed tithing (Matt. 23:23; Luke 11:42, 18:12; Heb. 7:1-21).

E.   Tithing reminds us that_____ we have comes from the Lord (Deut. 8:11, 17-18).

F.   Tithing is a cure for our_____ (Matt. 6:19-21).

GENEROSITY BRINGS BLESSING

A.   "A generous man will himself be_____" (Prov. 22:9).

B.   God blesses us so we can be a blessing to_____ (2 Cor. 9:8).

C.   The Early Church_____ to those in need and the Lord added to their number (Acts 4:32, 6:7).

AVOIDING THE MISUSE OF FINANCES

A.   "A greedy man brings_____ to his family" (Prov. 15:27). The Bible warns us to avoid the trap of greed (1 Tim. 6:6-10; Ps. 62:10). A rich young ruler had kept all the commandments of God, but Jesus told him he lacked one thing, so he had to _____ and "You will have treasure in Heaven" (Luke 18:18-25).

B.   Peter told Jesus, "We have left everything to follow You." Jesus replied, "No-one who has left home or brothers or sisters or mother or father or children or fields for Me and the Gospel will fail to receive_____ as much in this present age.......and in the age to come, eternal life" (Mark 10:28-30).

C.   "Give, and it will be_____ to you....For with the measure you use, it will be measured to you" (Luke 6:38).

D.   "Command those who are rich in this present world not to be arrogant nor to put their hope in wealth ....and to be_____ and willing to share" (1 Tim. 6:17-19).

E. "Be on your guard against all kinds of greed" (Luke 12:15). Life does not consist of 'things'.

F. Scripture tells us not to store up treasures on Earth, but to store up treasures in Heaven (Matt. 6:19-21). God does not need our money, but He wants our hearts (Matt. 6:21).

G. A rich man gave a huge amount, but a widow gave a very small amount. But she gave more – how is this possible? Because the rich man gave out of his abundance, but the widow gave all she had (Luke 21:1-3).

> God blesses us so that we might be a blessing to others
> (Gen. 22:17-18; 1 Chr. 4:10; 2 Cor. 9:8).

WHAT IS A FIRST FRUIT?

A. The first is the best part to give to the Lord: if I am expecting 20 barrels of apples next year in my harvest, then my promise is to give God the first portion.

B. Once a year, the people of God would bring their first fruits and no-one was to come empty-handed (Ex. 23:16 and 19, 34:22).

C. Honour the Lord with the_____ of_____ your crops, then your barns will overflow. Thus giving a first fruit demonstrates a belief in God for an increase and an abundance in the coming year.

D. Jesus was the_____. Just as in Adam we all die, in Christ we are made alive (1 Cor. 15:20-24). Jesus was the first part of what was to follow. Salvation for all those who are saved was made possible because of what Christ did at the first.

WHY THE FIRST PART?

A. Whatever we do with the first determines what will happen to the rest. If the first part is holy, then the rest is holy. If the root is holy, so are the branches (Rom: 11:16).

B. First fruits bring blessings to our household and protection over our family (Ezek. 44:30).

WHAT IS THE DIFFERENCE BETWEEN A FIRST FRUIT AND A TITHE?

First fruits is thanking the Lord for blessing and protection for the future harvest. First fruits is putting God above everything else and is given for the expected increase that is to come in the next twelve months.

A tithe is for God to meet our present needs and to protect what we have now.

- A. A tithe is a command: God says that we_____ from Him if we do not tithe (Mal. 3:8).
- B. Withholding a tithe brings us under a_____ (Mal. 3:9).
- C. Withholding a tithe is like earning a wage and putting it in a purse with holes in it (Hag. 1:6).
- D. So tithing is a command and a protection: it is a tenth of our income.

However, first fruits is more powerful than the tithe as it protects the following year.

FIRST FRUITS IS AN ISSUE OF FAITH

We have to learn that first fruits is both:
- A. A faith to give.
- B. A faith to receive.

God spoke to Moses and told him, "When you enter the land I am going to give you and reap its harvest, bring to the priest a sheaf of the first grain that you harvest. He is to wave the sheaf before the Lord" (Lev. 23:9-11).

First fruits was given on the first day after the Sabbath, which was when Jesus, the First Fruit, rose from the dead. All those who are now saved and being saved are the direct result of Christ the First Fruit. "He was delivered over to death for our sins and was raised to life for our justification" (Rom. 4:25).

- A. In tithes, offerings and first fruits, we give with a_____ heart (2 Cor. 9:7).
- B. We give_____ (Heb. 13:16).
- C. We give_____ (2 Cor. 8:3 and 12).
- D. We give_____ (2 Cor. 8:2 and 13).
- E. We give_____ (2 Cor. 9:11).

Tithes, offerings and first fruits release people and Churches to do what God has called them to do. They are given in order to reach the nations and, if understood correctly, Churches would explode with growth because there would be sufficient resources to do the work at hand. Tremendous blessing would be seen both naturally and supernaturally.

Chapter 14
LOYALTY & FAITHFULNESS

14. LOYALTY & FAITHFULNESS

Today, Church can attract many people with little understanding about how to live in right relationships. People will often come looking for a platform on which to preach, or to find some position or to be recognised for some gifting that they feel they may have.

Scripture tells us that it is not honourable to seek one's own honour (Prov. 25:27).

In our subconscious, fallen nature, we can use each other and the Church to further our own reputation or ministry, and if it does not work out, then we simply leave.

"Many a man claims to have unfailing love, but a faithful man who can find?"
(Prov. 20:6).

The nation of Israel made covenants with God and man, but God said that they were like Adam who broke the covenant with Him and were unfaithful (Hos. 6:4-7).

> God expects loyalty, even when He does things differently to the way we would expect. When Church Leaders and friends do things differently to the way we expect, the Lord still desires us to be faithful and loyal to them. Things being done differently to the way in which we would do them does not necessarily mean they are wrong: they are just different.

WHAT IS LOYALTY?

A. Loyalty is a_____, not a feeling.

B. Loyalty makes us_____ on others.

C. Loyalty is a_____ to develop friendship.

D. Loyalty is an_____ which affects our thinking and lifestyle.

E. Loyalty is at a_____ as we become vulnerable with friends (Prov. 27:6).

F. Loyalty is a_____ as we are connected to imperfect men.

G. Loyalty is a_____, with no plans to exit when we do not get our own way.

H. Loyalty is sticking together in the_____ times and the_____ times (Prov. 24:10). Prov. 17:17 advises us, "A friend loves at all times and a brother is born for adversity".

WHAT ARE THE REWARDS OF LOYALTY?

A. Loyalty refreshes the spirit of Leaders (Prov. 25:13).

B. Loyalty gives greater strength to the Church (Ecc. 4:9-12).

C. Loyalty allows the Spirit of the Lord to be poured out (Ps. 133:1). Oil in the Old Testament is symbolic of the Holy Spirit. When there is unity, faithfulness and loyalty, it brings a pleasant atmosphere into the Lord's Church.

D. God hates dissension (Prov. 6:16 and 19). But loyalty overlooks our weaknesses (Prov. 10:12).

E. Loyalty is a decision to remain in the Church family, whatever situation occurs. We are to be_____ in the House of the Lord (Ps. 1:3; Jer. 17:8). In this scripture, a tree planted by the water has roots, and all this is symbolic of the Spirit of God (Ps. 92:13-14). Stay planted in the House of the Lord, and then you will flourish when you are old, still producing good fruit and staying fresh and green.

WHAT EFFECTS DOES DISLOYALTY HAVE?

A. The_____ are_____ by their duplicity, but integrity guides us (Prov.11:3).

B. Disloyalty is destructive to our relationships (Gal. 5:15).

C. Unfaithfulness is like a bad_____: it brings pain to the body (Prov. 25:19).

D.   It brings displeasure from God (Prov. 6:19; Gal. 5:20-21).

E.   Paul experienced disloyalty and said it did him a great deal of_____
     (2 Tim. 4:14).

F.   We are given guidelines on how to deal with a disloyal and divisive person: we
     warn them twice and then have_____ to do with them. Such is the
     destructiveness of disloyalty (Titus 3:10).

G.   Disloyalty is contagious, so Solomon says in Prov. 12:26, 22:24-25, choose your
     friends_____.

H.   Disloyalty and trouble can come out of wanting to know what is going on when it
     has nothing to do with us (Ps. 131:1; 1 Thess. 4:11; 1 Tim. 5:13).

I.   Disloyalty to your own Church can come out of chasing other teaching not in line
     with what your own Leaders have taught, and so you have a mixture of belief.
     This can weaken the Church. Scripture tells us that if we do this and_____
     the_____, we will get a weak harvest (Deut. 22:9).

Loyalty should be expressed to those Leaders over you, even when they fail you.
Loyalty should be expressed to those over you when they come under accusation.

If God's people have a revelation on loyalty and faithfulness, the House of the Lord
becomes the happiest, the most secure and the most fulfilling place to be on the
whole Earth.

CHAPTER 15

GIFTS OF THE SPIRIT

15. GIFTS OF THE SPIRIT

Gifts of the Spirit are often misunderstood. So in this lesson, we are going to look at the gifts and their function in the Local church.

"There are different kinds of gifts, but the same Spirit. There are different kinds of service, but the same Lord. There are different kinds of working, but the same God works all of them in all men. Now to each one the manifestation of the Spirit is given for the common good" (1 Cor. 12: 4-7).

WHAT KINDS OF GIFTS ARE GIVEN?

Nine gifts are mentioned in 1 Cor. 12:8-11:

Three Gifts of the Mind: Wisdom, Knowledge, Discerning of Spirits   - MIND
Three Gifts of the Mouth: Tongues, Interpretation, Prophecy   - MOUTH
Three Gifts of Action: Faith, Healing, Miracles   - ACTION

GIFTS OF THE MIND

    A.   The word of <u>Wisdom</u> provides answers beyond man's_____ to solve.

    B.   Wisdom came upon Solomon in a situation with a mother who was an imposter (1 Kings 3:16-28).

    C.   Wisdom came upon Jesus when the Pharisees sought to trap Him when a woman was caught in an adulterous situation (John 8:6). He could have given either of two answers:

        - if Jesus obeyed the Law, the woman should have been stoned to death;

        - if Jesus came from a position of mercy, He would be disobeying the Law.

He finally gave an answer: "If any one of you is without sin, let him be the first to throw a stone at her" (John 8:7).

Several attempts to trap Jesus failed because of the gift of Wisdom (Matt. 17:24-27, 22:21).

D.   Wisdom extends the boundaries of understanding beyond our own capability.

E.   <u>Knowledge</u> is information from God. Peter knew Ananias had_____ (Acts 5:3). Other examples include: John 1:48, 4:18, 6:15; Luke 5:22; Acts 10:19-21, 14:9.

F.   <u>Discerning of Spirits</u> helps to identify the_____ behind the activity, whether it is holy, human or demonic.

G.   False prophets are recognised (Matt. 7:15-16).

H.   Jesus saw a spirit of infirmity in the disabled woman (Luke 13:11-12), and Paul discerned a spirit in a girl (Acts 16:16-18).

GIFTS OF THE MOUTH

A.   <u>Tongues</u> is a God-given ability to speak in an unknown language (Acts 2:1-7).

B.   <u>Interpretation</u> is the ability to exclaim the wonders of God (Acts 2:11). This is not prophecy, but the interpretation of a tongue that declares all the amazing attributes of God (1 Cor. 14:2). The interpretation is to_____, and not to man.

C.   Paul said, "I would like every one of you to speak in tongues" (1 Cor. 14:5), meaning it is possible for all to speak in tongues, or everyone has the potential.

D.   <u>Prophecy</u> is the ability to speak out a message from God, which is given by the Holy Spirit.

E.   Unlike speaking in a tongue, which is from man to God (1 Cor. 14:2), prophecy is from God to man (1 Cor. 14:3).

F.   Prophecy comes from the Greek word *propheteuo*, primarily meaning 'telling forth divine counsels'. This is not the same as preaching, though both of them are inspired by the Holy Spirit.

G.   There are three levels of prophecy: i) all may prophesy (1 Cor. 14:31); ii) the gift of prophecy (1 Cor. 12:10); iii) the ministry of the prophet (1 Cor. 12:28).

> Philip's daughters prophesied, but then along came Agabus who was more specific and it was clear that a different gifting was needed (Acts 21:8-11).

H.   Being able to prophesy does not make you a prophet.

I.   We prophesy according to the proportion of our faith (Rom. 12:6).

GIFTS OF ACTION

A. Faith, or having the gift of Faith, is greater than the level of normal faith. We are saved through faith (Eph. 2:8), but the gift of Faith comes when we believe God for an impossible task (Ex. 14:13, 21-22; Acts 3:11-16). It is a gift of additional Faith (Mark 11:22-23).

B. The Gift of Healing is an ability given by God to impart healing to the physical body at specific times (Acts 28:8-10).

C. Working of Miracles is something supernatural that occurs beyond what is natural. A miracle denotes a change in the natural laws.

D. The Gospels record nine miracles that Jesus performed:

   i) Water to wine (John 2:9);

   ii) Feeding of the 5000 (Matt. 14:13-21);

   iii) Feeding of the 4000 (Mark 8:6);

   iv) A great haul of fish (Luke 5:6);

   v) Walking on water (Matt. 14:25);

   vi) Calming the storm (Mark 4:41);

   vii) Calmed the storm (Mark 6:51);

   viii) Cursing the fig tree (Matt. 21:18-19);

   ix) A great catch of fish (John 21:6).

WHAT IS THE PURPOSE OF THE GIFTS?

A. The gifts always_____ the Church and never pull down
   (1 Cor. 14:3-5, 12 and 17-26).
   BUT A WORD OF CAUTION

B. Is it the right time? (Ecc. 3:1-8).

C. Is my_____ correct? (3 John:9).

> Using the gifts does not signify God's approval of an individual or a Church. Paul spoke to the Church in Corinth about the gifts as they were freely used. But the people themselves were corrupt: gifts can be misused (Matt. 7:21-23).

Gifts can be used in a presumptuous way: when the Israelites crossed the Red Sea, the Egyptians also believed they could do the same. However, this was not founded on the will of God, and so the result was that the whole of the Egyptian army drowned (Ex. 14:23-28).

HOW DO WE FUNCTION IN THESE GIFTS?

A. The Holy Spirit will do His_____ (1 Cor. 12:11, 18 and 28), but He never forces.

B. We should be totally_____ to Jesus (Rom. 6:1-2 and 13).

C. We should have a_____ to be used (1 Cor.14:1).

D. Find out_____ we can about the gifts (1 Cor. 12:1).

E. Seek the Lord and_____ to function in this area (1 Cor.12:31).

F. Use the gifts in_____ to our faith (Rom. 12:6; Mark 6:5-6).

G. Don't_____ the gifts (1 Tim. 4:14; 2 Tim. 1:6).

WHAT CAUTIONS DO WE PUT IN PLACE?

A. Misuse of the gifts of the Spirit has done much harm to the Church of the Lord Jesus Christ through imbalance, which the Lord abhors (Prov. 11:1, 16:11, 20:23).

B. So a good balance is the Lord's delight (Prov. 11:1).

C. We balance the gifts of the Spirit with the fruit of the Spirit, which is: Love, Joy, Peace, Patience, Kindness, Goodness, Faithfulness, Gentleness and Self-Control. So we live by the Spirit and keep in step with the Spirit (Gal. 5:22-23 and 25).

D. If it is all Spirit, we blow up: gifts of the Spirit must be balanced with the fruit of the Spirit. Gifts are instant so they can be used by immature people: fruit is cultivated over time.

E. Correctly balanced gifts are given so that the Church can move in a supernatural way to reach those who do not know the Lord Jesus Christ, and are given to build God's Church on Earth.

F. The Church is the_____ and_____ of the truth (1 Tim. 3:15).

The Church is the greatest place on Earth, so seek the best gifts to build His Church and then you will have fulfilment and joy in making His Church great.

CHAPTER 16
THE ACT OF WORSHIP

16. THE ACT OF WORSHIP

There are many religious groups who appear to have different forms of worship. Some have said that God has made the various ways to suit our varying personalities. However, this is incorrect. There is only one way to worship and that is 'The Bible Way', using the principles that have been given to us by God Himself.

HOW ARE WE TO WORSHIP?

A.   True worshippers are to worship in_____ and in_____ (John 4:21-24).

B.   If there is true worship, there must also be false worship. False worship is often just_____ taught by men (Is. 29:13; Mark 7:6-9).

C.   God promised that He would_____ David's fallen tent (Amos 9:11; Acts 15:15-16).

D.   David's tent was a physical demonstration of the spiritual act of worship (Rom. 12:1, 1 Pet. 2:5). It was based on a principle that God ordained to show His people the correct way to enter into His holy presence. Its blueprint took the form of this simple illustration:

i)   The Outer Court with a brazen altar is where the priest would cleanse himself;

ii)   He would then move on into the Holy Place which was lit by oil lamps;

iii)   He would then move into the Holy of Holies which had no oil lamps or artificial light, but was lit by God's shining glory. In this place was the Ark of the Covenant which represented God's holy presence;

iv)   Such was the presence of God that sometimes the priest could not function (2 Chr. 5:14).

HOW DOES THIS AFFECT US TODAY?

A.   Scripture tells us that as humans, we are made up of_____, _____ and_____ (1 Thess. 5:23).

B.   We are made in the image of God (Gen. 1:26), who is Father, Son and Holy Spirit. Three parts to the blueprint of the tent, three parts to us, three parts to God.

OUR BODY

A.   Our bodies reflect the Outer Court. So after a pre-prayer time to wash ourselves, we come into the Outer Court with_____ (Ps. 100:4).

B.   Praising (Ps. 34:1, 40:16, 42:4, 66:8).

C.   Singing (Ps. 5:11, 32:11, 47:6, 61:8, 68:4, 104:33).

D.   Shouting (Ps. 35:27; 1 Chr. 15:28; Is. 12:6).

E.   Clapping (Ps. 47:1, 98:8; Is. 55:12).

F.   Dancing (1 Chr. 15:29; 2 Sam. 6:14; Ps. 149:3, 150:4).

G.   Lifting of hands (Ps. 63:4, 119:48, 134:2).

H.   With instruments (1 Chr. 23:5, 25:1-7; Ps. 33:2-3, 57:8, 150:3-6).

I.   Thanking God (1 Chr. 16:4, 8 and 41).

J.   Praise is 'the_____ of our lips' (Heb. 13:15).

OUR SOUL

A.   Our souls reflect the Holy Place, a place where our emotions are involved – tears, joy, appreciation for who God is.

B.   "My_____ will rejoice in the Lord" (Ps. 35:9).

C.   "My soul_____ for you, O God" (Ps. 42:1).

D.   "Praise the Lord, O my soul" (Ps. 103:1-2, 104:35).

God created us with emotions which reflect the Holy Place.

OUR SPIRIT

A.   After our soul has encountered the Lord God, most Churches would stop there. But the principle is that we move on into His shining glory, the Holy of Holies.

B.   In the Holy of Holies, we ascribe to the Lord the glory due to His name (1 Chr. 16:29) and we worship Him in the splendour of His holiness.

C.   The Greek word for worship is *proskuneo*, which means 'to make obeisance, an act of homage or reverence to God'.

D.   Worship is the total surrender of our lives to God as we were created to praise Him (Is. 43:21). "I will praise you with_____ of my heart."

E.   The tent of David is not physically being brought back, but our bodies are now the place where God dwells (1 Cor. 6:19).

F.   Battles are won when we enter the Holy of Holies (2 Chr. 20:21-22). Miracles can happen and a supernatural release can occur in true worship.

G.   True worship can make us uncomfortable when we are not in a good place with God (Matt. 21:15-16).

H.   Worship can bring God back into the centre of our lives and give us peace (Is. 26:3).

WORSHIPPING CHURCHES ARE HAPPY CHURCHES

A.   Jesus comes into the centre of worshippers (Matt. 18:20).

B.   Jesus loves us and sings our praises in the congregation (Heb. 2:11-12; Ps. 22:22). God is not seeking worship, but worshippers.

C.   The Old Testament reveals what will be in the New (Ps. 102:18).

D.   The Old was written for a future generation so they may_____ the Lord. Rev. 4:10-11 says that God created all things, and that includes worship.

The primary purpose of our salvation is to worship God and nothing else can satisfy the longing of the heart. So do not wait until the Spirit moves you to worship as you will wait a very long time. Worship is an act of the will. David said, "I WILL praise the Lord!" (Ps. 16:7, 26:12, 34:1, 145:1).

CHAPTER 17

THE HOME: GOD'S DESIGN

17. THE HOME: GOD'S DESIGN

These days when the home is mentioned, all kinds of definitions are given to describe it. But God has a design for the home and families. Not only is God restoring His Church, but He is also restoring homes and families (Ps. 127:1-5; Mal. 4:5-6).

This lesson is not meant to make single parents, the divorced or those in circumstances inhibiting family life feel uncomfortable, but it is to look at God's design according to the Bible. In fact, the House of God is a great place for people who are not in a family (Ps. 68:6). God sets the_____ into families.

GOD BUILDS THE HOUSE

A.   God gives the wisdom to build (Prov. 14:1; Ps. 127:1).

B.   As in the natural, so it is in the spiritual.

C.   God is our Father (Ps. 68:5; Is. 64:8).

D.   As in the natural, God provides seed that brings about our birth (1 Pet. 2:2-3).

E.   In Church, we have an Elder Brother, the Lord Jesus (Heb. 2:14-17).

F.   We have an Elder Son over His House (Heb. 3:6).

G.   There is a first-born in the spiritual family (Rom. 8:29).

H.   God is the Father with His family (John 1: 12-13, 3:13; 1 Pet. 1:23).

I.   We have the same blood (John 6:53).

J.   We take the family name (Eph. 3:14-15).

K.   We have the family resemblance or image (1 Cor. 15:49).

L.   We have spiritual fathers, mothers, brothers and sisters in a defined family membership.

GOD'S ORDER IN THE HOME

A.   The man is the_____ of the home (1 Cor. 11:3; Eph. 5:23-25).

B.   This does not make the woman inferior as both are equal, like Christ who is equal with God, but who made Himself subject to God (1 Cor. 15:28).

C.   The man is not to be a dictator, but to love his wife as himself (Eph. 5:28; Col. 3:19).

> If the role of headship is confused, it will cause problems.

D.   Eve assumed the lead role by taking the forbidden fruit. Adam abdicated his responsibility as head of the family. Adam and Eve were thrown out of the Garden of Eden and so sin came into the world (Gen. 3:1-24).

E.   Eve took the lead, but God blamed the man (Gen. 3:17; Rom. 5:12).

F.   Jezebel took the lead in Naboth's murder, but God blamed the husband (1 Kings 21:1-19).

G.   Role confusion can affect future generations (1 Kings 22:51-53; 2 Chr. 21:5-6, 22:10-12). Ultimately, the man is held accountable.

H.   The man will rule over a woman (Gen. 3:17; 1 Cor. 11:3).

THE MAN IS TO BE RIGHTLY SUBMITTED TO GOD

A.   Christ must be the man's_____ (1 Cor. 11:3).

B.   The man must be a good_____ (1 Tim. 5:8; Ex. 12:3).

C.   The man must be a source of_____ (Eph. 5:25; Col. 3:19).

D.   The man must treat his wife with_____ (1 Pet. 3:7; Eph. 5:29).

E.   The man must be considerate and respect the woman, otherwise his_____ will be hindered (1 Pet. 3:7).

THE ROLE OF THE WOMAN

A.   Allow her husband to be the head and receive his_____ (1 Cor. 11:3; Eph. 5:22-24).

B.   Honour her husband (1 Pet. 3:6).

C.   Have a good attitude and a_____, gentle spirit (1 Pet. 3:1-5).

D.   A supporter of her husband (Gen. 2:18).

E.   A woman given to_____ (Heb. 13:1-2).

THE ROLE OF CHILDREN

A. Parents are to_____ their children (Deut. 4:9-10; Prov. 22:6; Eph. 6:4).

B. Eli did not_____ his sons, which had serious consequences (1 Sam. 3:11-13).

C. In the Oxford English Dictionary, the definition of 'to train' is 'guiding mental and moral development, to bring up, to condition, to prepare, to make fit'.

D. Children are to be_____ (Prov. 23:13-14, 29:15 and 17).

WHY TRAIN CHILDREN?

A. i) They are sinners; ii) they lack knowledge; iii) they are vulnerable.

B. Parents train by example just as their_____ will be passed on to the children by their example (Ex. 20:5-6; Lam. 5:7).

C. It is the parents'_____ (Deut. 11:18-21; Eph. 6:4).

D. Training children protects them from negative world influences; if parents don't train, then children will receive training from other sources.

E. We are exhorted to obey our parents (Eph. 6:1-3).

CHILDREN ARE GIFTS FROM GOD

A. They are a_____ of the Lord (Ps. 127:3-5).

B. They are the Lord's_____ (Ps.127:3).

C. They are a_____ (Prov. 17:6).

WHAT MAKES A GOOD FAMILY?

Men play a key role in ensuring a happy family environment. However, there is no instant formula for a good home. But if, to the best of our abilities, we place God's design for the family into all the family members, then that will give the Lord a doorway into blessing that family unit.

A. By keeping good attitudes (Phil. 2:5).

B. Love is not a feeling, but a lifestyle. If we practise this in the family, then problems will be much less in that family (1 Cor. 13:4-7).

C.   We must learn to forgive; and we will have plenty of opportunity to put that principle into practice (Matt. 18:23-35).

D.   Do not make 'Me' the centre of my family, but place OTHERS above ME (Phil. 2:3).

E.   Be transparent, have openness and maintain clear communication, all of which build the family. Keep away from negativity (Eph. 4:29).

Homes can be filled with all the joy God has promised if we live according to His design. Or we can ignore God's plan, which then potentially can make a home unpleasant and joyless. Every believer should work hard to make home a place of fun, peace, joy and fulfilment (Rom. 14:17).

FINALLY – GOD'S PROTECTION OVER THE HOME

A.   God gave Moses instructions that if the Israelites sacrificed a lamb and sprinkled its blood over their door-posts, then the plague striking down the Egyptians would pass over their households (Ex. 12:21-23).

B.   But a warning came with this promise, that they had to "_____ these instructions as a lasting ordinance for you and your descendants" (Ex. 12:24).

C.   So one key to happy family life is obedience to God's Word. Then we can enjoy all the benefits of God's protection and live in the joy and fruitfulness of family life.

CHAPTER 18

THE CHURCH: GOD'S ETERNAL PURPOSE

18. THE CHURCH: GOD'S ETERNAL PURPOSE

The Bible says that the Lord is building His Church and that Hades will not overcome it (Matt. 16:18). But what is Church? Many today have little understanding of the amazing plan and purpose God has had for this incredible organism since the beginning of time (Matt. 16:18-19).

WHAT IS THE CHURCH?

A.   Church is the_____ _____ of God (Eph. 1:9-10). Eph. 5:32 says that the Church is a profound mystery, which it was to the Jews, who were blind to it.

B.   Church is a new_____ nation, neither Jew nor Gentile (1 Cor. 10:32). God is working on a third group, baptising Jew and Gentile alike into one Body (Eph. 2:11-22; 1 Cor. 12:13; 1 Pet. 2:9).

C.   Church is a place of_____ from false Christs and ministries, as well as against the tide of darkness; it is like an umbrella in the rain, covering us from Satan's darts (Ps. 91:1-16; Is. 4:2-6, 59:19; Matt. 24:4).

D.   The Church is God's instrument, which He desires to use to extend His Kingdom (Matt. 21:43; Eph. 1:3-14, 3:9-11).

E.   Church is a_____ with a Father (Ps. 68:5; Is. 64:8).

F.   Church is a place where we have an Elder_____ (Rom. 8:29; Heb. 2:14-17, 3:6).

G.   Church is a place where we take the family_____ (Eph. 3:14-15).

H.   In Church, we have a family image (1 Cor. 15:49).

On the other hand:

A. Church is not a_____. In the Greek, it is the *ekklesia* meaning 'called-out' or 'the called-out ones'.

B. Church is not an_____ of Judaism. All the ceremonialism of Judaism was abolished at the cross.

C. Church is not a_____ or a_____, which cause only fights and quarrels (1 Cor. 3:1-4).

D. Church is not an individual, but an_____ group of people (Acts 2:41).

THE CHURCH IS ALWAYS TOGETHER

A. Paul talks about the Church together (1 Cor. 14:23). There are further references to this (see Acts 20:7, 14:27; Heb. 10:25; 1 Pet. 2:4-10; 1 John 1:3).

B. Church is a family (Eph. 3:15).

Some try to live in many families, but this causes problems. If a father said he had a family called Smith with whom he lived this month, and then lived with one called Brown the next month, and then with the Adams family sometimes, he would have a messy life. However, many treat the Church this way. God intended us to have just one family, where we commit our resources and efforts. But, we can be friendly with other families.

C. Some treat their Local Church like a club and change it when they tire; or like an old cloth which is thrown away when finished with.

D. In Eph. 5:22-33, Paul talks about how a marriage should work and how to treat each other. But then in verse 32 he says, "I am talking about Christ and the Church."

E. The attitude we have to our Church and how we treat it reflects on how we treat Christ and our attitude to Him.

THE UNIVERSAL CHURCH

A. The Church all over the world is called 'The Universal Church'. Even those from the past are part of this amazing group.

B. When believers around the world suffer, then we also suffer (Acts 11:27-30; 1 Cor. 12:26).

C. The Worldwide Church is more than a denomination or group: it consists of every nation, every tribe and every language (2 Pet. 3:9; Rev. 5:9-10, 14:6-7).

THE LOCAL CHURCH

Although the Universal Church is important, it is referred to in the Bible just 10% of the time. On the other hand, the Local Church is spoken about 90% of the time. So God puts the greater emphasis on the Local Church, and what God emphasises, we must also emphasise.

A.   The Local Church is where we work out the principles of relationship, covenant and friendship (Matt. 18:15-35).

B.   The Local Church is the place where God matures us (Eph. 4:11-16).

C.   The Local Church is where our function and purpose is worked out (Rom. 12:3-8; 1 Cor. 12:18-28).

D.   We put our roots down in the Local Church (Ps. 1:3). The root determines what kind of fruit is produced. If you pull a plant out of the soil, it soon withers.

E.   Is. 55:12 says that all the trees clap their hands and will go out in joy; the term 'trees' in the scripture refers to people.

F.   Jer. 17:7-8 describes us as trees 'planted by the water'. This scripture refers to the tough times when we will remain strong, if planted in God's House. Reference to roots means we are to stay where we are planted; the streams refer to the Holy Spirit, while the trunk is our character which in turn nurtures fruit in our branches. So the Local Church is extremely important to God.

THE CHURCH IS ALSO CALLED

A.   The Pillar and Foundation of Truth (1 Tim. 3:15).

B.   God's Household (1 Tim. 3:15; Heb. 3:1-4).

C.   The Temple that is Holy (Eph. 2:21-22).

D.   The Bride of Christ (Eph. 5: 28-32; Rev. 19:6-9).

E.   The Army of God (Eph. 6:10-13; 2 Tim. 2:3-4).

F.   The Family of God (Eph. 3:14-15).

G.   The House of Faith (Gal. 6:10 AV).

H.   The Body of Christ (Eph. 1:20-23).

ARE PARA-CHURCH GROUPS THE SAME AS A CHURCH?

There are many Christian groups outside of the Local Church who do good work, but they are there because in times past the Church did not function as it was meant to. So para-church organisations such as men's and women's networks, evangelistic organisations, Bible Colleges and many other ministries arose. All did what the Church did not do.

God is now bringing His Church back to a place where it functions in the way it was intended, with men's and women's groups, evangelism, training of young people in the Bible, missions work, business-people's groups, and much more flowing out of the Church. As the Lord's Church gets stronger, so para-church will be needed less and less as time goes by.

GOD IS NOW BUILDING HIS CHURCH

    A.   The Church is going to be_____ (Eph. 5:23-32).

    B.   The Church is going to_____ (Matt. 16:18-19) and be_____ (Rom. 16:20).

    C.   The Church will be without_____ or_____ or any other_____ (Eph. 5:27).

        Not all Christians are to be found in the Local Church. Some are outside because of hurt, or lack of understanding. Perhaps they are outside the Church because they have a rebellious nature or an independent spirit, or they have picked up an offence. Whatever, God's plan is for all to be in His Church. Here, they can find restoration and be involved once more in His blueprint, which is the Church, the most exciting, amazing, awesome and incredible organisation on the face of the Earth.

    D.   Do not give up_____ together, as some are in the habit of doing (Heb. 10:25).

CHAPTER 19
THE RESTORED CHURCH

19. THE RESTORED CHURCH

Acts 3:19-21 talks about Jesus remaining in Heaven until the restoration of all that God promised through the Old Testament prophets. It is the most joyful and exciting experience for believers once they begin to catch in these promises a glimpse of God's purpose for His Church. So we shall look at what the prophets have said.

In Acts 15:15-18, the disciples of Christ began to get excited about this plan of God.

A.   In verse 15, they noted that events unfolding were in agreement with the prophets, and in verse 18, that such things had been known for ages.

B.   The disciples referred to what Amos the prophet had said when he used the word 'restore' (Amos 9:11).

What does 'restore' mean? The Concise Oxford English Dictionary defines it as, 'to bring back to the original state by rebuilding or repairing'. So when it is applied to the Church, it means 'to recover truth that has been lost'.

WHAT WAS LOST IN THE CHURCH?

The Church today is a pale shadow of what it was intended to be in the New Testament, so we shall look at what was lost first:

100AD	The gifting of the Apostles disappeared.
130AD	Laying on of hands became a ritual.
140AD	The gifts of the Prophet fell into disuse.
160AD	Plurality of Elders was no longer practised.

187AD	The first infant baptism was recorded.
200AD	Worship became a ritual without the Holy Spirit.
210AD	The priesthood of believers was not taught, and one man ran the Church.
225AD	Membership was not based on salvation, but by agreeing with the Creed.
350AD	Christianity was made the state religion by Emperor Constantine.
380AD	Rome was made the final authority on all Church matters.
400AD	From here on, this was known as 'The Dark Ages of the Church'.

I WILL RESTORE EVERYTHING (ACTS 3:21, 15:16)

1517AD	God breathed on Martin Luther who began to preach faith in Jesus.
1524AD	A group called the Anabaptists began baptising by full immersion.
1700AD	In Moravia, now part of the Czech Republic, another group started to pray: this prayer revival group was called the Moravians.
1750AD	God revealed another lost truth, this time to John Wesley who preached sanctification. In this revival, the Wesley brothers wrote over 6,000 hymns.
1800AD	Some people had a revelation about the return of Jesus and began Bible studies: they were called Brethren. At the same time, William Booth founded the Salvation Army: he preached 'Go for souls and go for the worst', and thus social concern was born.
1900AD	Baptism in the Holy Spirit was restored.
1906AD	In Azuza Street, San Francisco, California, the gifts of the Spirit manifested for the first time in almost 2,000 years.
1923AD	The Pentecostal Revival all over the world saw people filled with the Holy Spirit.
1948AD	In Canada, spontaneous praise and worship was restored.
1965AD	Individuals in different denominations began to be filled with the Holy Spirit in what was the beginning of the Charismatic Movement.
1973AD	The message of Restoration was heard around the world.

WHAT IS BEING RESTORED TO THE CHURCH?

A.   _____ that was lost (Acts 3:21).

B.   _____; that is to say, there will be men who will deal righteously with sin (Is. 1:21-27).

C.   _____ that the prophets have promised (Acts 3:21).

D.   _____ who will direct people to the Word of God, not psychology (Is. 1:26).

E.   _____ of the Word, who will explain the Bible correctly (Is. 30:20).

F.   _____ will be made whole again (Mal. 4:6).

G.   The_____ of the _____ will attract many people: it will no longer be the tail, but established and recognised for its importance in the world (Deut. 28:13; Is. 2:2).

H.   Tabernacle of David_____ restored, also called Davidic worship (Amos 9:11).

I.   An_____ of the Holy Spirit, as experienced by the Early Church, will be combined with another outpouring in the Last Days. These two outpourings combined will be a double portion (Joel 2:23; James 5:7).

J.   _____ of the unconverted: Jesus talks about a dragnet collecting a great harvest across the world in the Last Days (Jer. 31:34; Matt. 13:47-49; Heb. 8:11).

K.   _____ and_____ will be evident (Jer. 30:17). In Matt.12:15, Jesus Himself healed all who came to Him and He promised that we would do even greater work than this (John 14:12).

A KEY PRINCIPLE OF GOD'S RESTORATION

A.   More is always given back (Ex. 22:1-3; Luke 19:18).

B.   Restoration is never a patch-up work, but it is always perfect and complete (Mark 3:5, 8:25).

C.   The glory of the_____ House will be greater than the former House. This was a prophecy of Haggai (Hag. 2:9-10) in the Septuagint (the Old Testament translated from Hebrew into Greek). So the End Time Church will be greater than the Early Church.

IS THE NATION OF ISRAEL PART OF THE END TIME CHURCH?

A. In the beginning, God created Adam to be an instrument of God (Gen. 1:27), but Adam failed.

B. God then chose a people called the Israelites to be the channel for His Kingdom and one through whom the Messiah would be born (Gal. 3:29).

C. Israel rejected the Messiah, so their branches were cut off from the Tree of Faith (Rom. 11:17-24). Adam failed and so too did Israel.

D. When Israel rejected the Messiah, God took the administration of the Kingdom from them and gave it to the Church (Matt. 21:43).

E. Now the Church of Jesus is the people of God and the new Israel (Gal. 6:16).

F. Whenever natural Jews receive Christ as their Saviour, they are grafted back on to the Tree of Faith. They become the new Israel. Both Jews and Gentiles are part of the Body of Christ (Eph. 2:11-22).

G. The Bible teaches that there WILL be a restoration of Israel when an outpouring of the Holy Spirit comes. It is NOT a restoration of Mosaic covenant ritualism (Joel 2:28-32; Acts 2:17; Rom. 10:1, 9-13, 11:23-26).

The Bible is a book of restoration from Genesis to Revelation. Man in Genesis failed God; then through Jesus, relationship with God was restored. God is going to complete His plan. The Grand Finale comes when the Church, the Bride of Christ, is ready and prepared for the return of the Lord Jesus Christ (Rev. 19:7).

The Bride (which is the Church) has made_____ ready. It is our responsibility to build an excellent and prepared Church – and WE can actually speed up that day! (2 Pet. 3:12).

CHAPTER 20

CHURCH GOVERNMENT

20. CHURCH GOVERNMENT

Church government has been abused or not implemented in the past. When it has been misused, some Christians want no repeat of that experience and so dispense with Church government altogether. Others do not put it into practice for fear of people leaving the Church. Yet, Church government is God's foundation for a balanced Church.

GOVERNMENT HAS BEEN ESTABLISHED BY GOD

A.   The Bible talks about government in the world, civil government, then government in our homes, and then government in the Church (Rom. 13:1-7; 1 Cor. 11:1-3; Heb. 13:17).

B.   God has established government in the_____ (Heb.13:17).

C.   God has established those who_____ in His House (Rom. 12:8).

WHO GOVERNS IN THE CHURCH?

A.   _____ rule in God's Church (1 Tim. 5:17).

B.   It is not rule by one man, but it is a_____ of Elders (Acts 14:23, 20:17; 1 Tim. 4:14; Titus 1:5; James 5:14).

C.   Note that Elders are not appointed just because the Bible advocates plurality, but because they are the right men (1 Tim. 3:1-9; Titus 1:5-9).

D.   A description of the office of an Elder:

OFFICE	GREEK WORD	DESCRIPTION	RECOGNITION
Elder	*Presbuteros*	Not a novice	Experienced
Bishop	*Episkopos*	Overseer	Carer
Chosen One	*Eklektos*	Chosen of God	Picked out

Of course, all Elders are not equal: there are varying degrees of experience, age and gifting. The scriptures emphasise the need for a Senior Leader, or a Set Man (Num. 27:15-23).

WHAT KIND OF PEOPLE ARE TO BE CHOSEN?

A. 1 Tim. 3:1-9 and Titus 1:5-9 tell us the kind of individual to be chosen.

B. He must have proven_____. Gifting alone is not the deciding factor.

He must have proven. Gifting alone is not the deciding factor.

If he has a weak character, he can bring disrepute to God's House.

C. He must be_____, not a novice; he must have the respect of non-Christians, be patient, and conduct an exemplary lifestyle.

D. Not only must an Elder be blameless, sober, not given to much wine, not greedy for money, not covetous or self-willed, but he must have a good_____, with his family in_____, his wife treated well, his children in obedience and his home hospitable.

E. An Elder must also have a measure of_____ or_____ to build up the believers. He can be an Apostle, Prophet, Evangelist, Pastor or Teacher, all part of the five-fold ministries described in Eph. 4:11-13.

HOW DO ELDERS FUNCTION WITH BELIEVERS?

A. They must be able to_____ or govern well. Having oversight of Church affairs, they are like spiritual parents in the Home (1 Thess. 5:12-14).

B. They must rule with_____, not ruling harshly (1 Pet. 5:3).

C. Elders must_____ the Church and be_____: they must guard against people who look like Christians, talk and act like Christians, but are destructive and divisive, often splintering groups from the Church (Acts 20:28-31).

D. Elders must be good_____ to the Church (1 Pet. 5:1-3).

E. They must not only handle the Word well, but must also be able to_____ with solid doctrine to bring maturity to the Church and help the Body to be released in its gifts and talents.

THE PEOPLE ALSO HAVE RESPONSIBILITIES TO THE ELDERS

Heb. 13:17 admonishes us to obey our Leaders. But is this purely to make their work-load lighter?

A. In Heb. 13:17, it is clear that those Elders keeping watch over the flock have to give an_____ to God for all they teach, instruct and guide.

B. We need to obey the Leaders so that their work will be a_____, not a burden, for that would be of no advantage to_____ (Heb. 13:17).

C. If we cause our Leaders trouble, they will not be able to function correctly and that is bad for the Church and for the individuals in it. On the other hand, if the work of the Elders is fulfilling and satisfying, then their greater ability to function brings greater advantages and benefits to both individuals and the Church as a whole.

D. In 1 Chr. 12, men came to join David in his stronghold. But he did not welcome them immediately. In verse 17, David said, "If you have come to me in peace, to help me, I am ready to have you unite with me."

E. In verse 18, Amasai said, "We are yours, O David." Note that he did not say, "We have come to help God". When individuals come into Church to help God, it is a misunderstanding of a principle. The responsibility of that individual is to support the Leaders.

F. Then Amasai wished David success, and "Success to those who help you, for your God will help you" (verse 18).

G. So as people in the Church accept their responsibility to support and help the Elders and make them successful, then the Church becomes successful and the people in it become successful too. So Heb. 13:17 is the same principle as 1 Chr. 12:18: obey your Leaders and bless them, and you also will be blessed and successful in the Kingdom.

H. We are to hold our Leaders in the highest_____ (1 Thess. 5:13).

I. We are to support them_____ (1 Tim. 5:17-18; 1 Cor. 9:11-14).

J. We are not hastily to accuse an Elder of wrongdoing (1 Tim. 5:1, 19-20).

K. We are to_____ for our Leaders (1 Thess. 5:25), for Elders are mortal men who have been set apart by God. They need all the prayer and help available.

L. Elders are worthy of_____ honour (1 Tim. 5:17-18).

It is the Lord's intention that the Elders and the people have good relationships. Where you find all in order, with good relationships and a happy atmosphere, there you will find a Church in harmony and with blessing, amongst both the Eldership and the people. Then the Church benefits from incredible strength to do what it is called to do, to "Go into all the world and preach the good news to all creation" (Mark 16:15).

CHAPTER 21

DISCIPLINE IN THE CHURCH

21. DISCIPLINE IN THE CHURCH

From the earliest conception of the Church, there have been individuals who have hurt it because of their independent spirit. Where you find a Church with little discipline, there you will find disorder and chaos. The Lord takes the natural to help us understand the spiritual: as the natural family without discipline would be chaotic, so it would be the same in the spiritual family. In a nation, you will also find principles of discipline.

Scripture clearly teaches discipline.

WHEN WOULD DISCIPLINE BE PUT INTO ACTION?

A.   Jesus gave us the principle of when discipline is needed. We are to proceed in accordance with Matt. 18:15-18: "If your brother sins against you, go and show him his fault, just between the_____ of you." No-one else should be told about the issue (v.15).

B.   If he will not listen, take_____ along so the matter may be established by the testimony of two or three witnesses (v.16).

C.   If he refuses to listen, tell it to the_____ (v.17).

D.   If he refuses to_____ even to the Church, then he is to be treated like a pagan or tax collector, the principle being to have nothing to do with him (v.17).

E.   The purpose of discipline is not to destroy, but as Paul said, it is like handing the offender over to Satan so that his sinful nature might be destroyed and his spirit saved on the Day of the Lord (1 Cor. 5:5), or so that he might understand he has_____ and repent of his wrongdoing.

DISCIPLINE IS NECESSARY BECAUSE:

A. It provides order in the Church and in the lives of people (Col. 3:5).

B. It gives understanding of right and wrong (1 Cor. 5:1-2).

C. Left to ourselves, some sin would not be dealt with (Gal. 6:1-2).

D. It opposes lawlessness (1 Tim. 1:9).

E. Sin can permeate the Church if left unchallenged (1 Cor. 5:6).

F. Without discipline, sin would continue and destroy any potential for God in people's lives.

G. Without discipline, others could follow the example of the undisciplined members.

H. Without discipline, respect for the Church and its Leaders evaporates.

I. To bring_____ to the individual (2 Cor. 7:10).

J. To keep the_____ of the Church (Rom. 2:24).

K. To bring the Church to a place where it is_____ and_____ (Eph. 5:27).

L. To bring the Church to a place where it is_____ (Eph. 5:27).

GOD'S ORDER FOR CHURCH IS LIKE A FAMILY

GOD HUSBAND – WIFE CHILDREN	SPIRITUAL AND NATURAL LAWS	GOD LEADERSHIP MEMBERS OF CHURCH

IN WHAT OTHER AREAS WOULD DISCIPLINE BE NECESSARY?

A. With false teaching or doctrine (Rom. 16:17; Titus 3:10-11).

B. When an individual claims to be a Christian, but persistently leads an immoral lifestyle or lives in a manner opposing scripture.

C. When an individual brings division into the Church, Paul urges us to keep away from such a person (Rom. 16:17; Titus 3:10). Often, Leaders talk and talk to the divisive ones to no avail while they continue to do more and more damage: scripture teaches us that after two warnings, we are to have nothing more to do with them.

D. With those that have a form of godliness (2 Tim. 3:5), but are not sincere.

E. With those who are idle and do not live according to the teaching (2 Thess. 3:6).

F. We are to keep away from gossips, idlers, busybodies, and those who do not obey instructions, so that they feel ashamed (2 Thess. 3:1-15).

G. With the sexually immoral (1 Cor. 5:9-11). In fact, the wicked man is to be expelled from the Church (v.13).

H. Those who continue in sin and go to different houses with gossip and slander accusing Elders without evidence, are to be publicly rebuked (1 Tim. 5:13-21).

Discipline may result in the expulsion of the individual from the Church, but scripture encourages us to appeal to the person to change his ways and adopt the Christ-like lifestyle that he professes. Scripture uses words like: correct (2 Tim. 3:16, 4:2); rebuke (2 Tim. 4:2); admonish (1 Thess. 5:12); and judge (1 Cor. 5:3 and 12-13).

THE ATTITUDE OF THOSE BRINGING DISCIPLINE MUST BE CHRIST-LIKE

A. He must be motivated by a godly passion (Eph. 4:15; Heb. 12:6; Rev. 3:19).

B. He must correct wisely (Prov. 25:12).

C. He must be ready to extend forgiveness and grace (2 Cor. 2:6-8).

D. He must have the heart of a father (1 Thess. 2:10-12).

E. He must have a spirit of humility (Gal. 6:1-2).

F. He must have a gentle spirit when correcting (Ps. 141:5; 1 Thess. 2:1-9).

G. He must have a desire to see repentance (Matt. 18:15).

FRUITS OF DISCIPLINE

No family can survive without discipline and no Church can survive without a balanced Church family disciplined in a godly manner.

A. _____ comes through discipline (Heb. 12:11).

B. Discipline is not pleasant at the time, but painful. Later on, however, it produces a_____ of righteousness and peace for those who have been trained by it (Prov. 15:10; Heb. 12:11).

Where discipline is functioning in a Church, it brings security to the members who know that any trouble will be dealt with in a godly manner. This releases freedom and joy, and a desire to bring others into the Church, where there is peace and harmony.

CHAPTER 22
CHURCH COMMITMENT

22. CHURCH COMMITMENT

Commitment is not a word that is found in the Bible, but the principle of commitment permeates the Word of God. For example, we do not find the words 'Trinity' or 'Rapture' in the Bible, but they are firmly established principles. No Church will reach its potential without a committed body of people.

The Concise Oxford English Dictionary defines commitment as 'the process or an instance of committing oneself; a pledge or an undertaking'.

A. A marriage is a commitment: when we are committed to someone, it means 'to cleave to', which in turn means 'to stick fast', 'to adhere to' or 'to join closely'.

B. The Lord seeks_____ to be committed and united (Gen. 2:24).

C. The Lord desires us to be firmly attached, or joined to_____ (Acts 11:23; 1 Cor. 6:17).

> If a man or a woman is only partially committed to the other, then the marriage will struggle and possibly fail. If individuals are only partially committed to their Church, then that Church will also struggle or fail.

D. Every natural family is committed to each other: in fact, it is the solution to_____ (Ps. 68:6).

E. The Church is God's family on Earth (Eph. 3:15; Gal. 6:10).

F. We are_____ upon each other (Eph. 4:16).

G. We are_____ of God's household (Eph. 2:19-22) and we are all being built together.

WE LIVE A LIFESTYLE OF COMMITMENT TO EACH OTHER

A.   By loving each other (1 Pet. 1:22).

B.   By praying for each other (James 5:16).

C.   We don't try to outclass anyone, but submit to each other (Eph. 5:21).

D.   If someone does a wrong to us, then we forgive him or her (Eph. 4:32).

E.   We give each other encouragement (1 Thess. 4:18).

F.   Our gifts are not for us to look good, but to serve each other (1 Pet. 4:10).

G.   We correct each other, which can save us from trouble (Col. 3:16).

H.   We aim to edify and to live in peace with each other (Rom. 14:19).

I.   We aim to encourage each other (Heb. 10:25).

THINGS TO AVOID AS CHRISTIANS

A.   Having a loose tongue and engaging in actions that hurt (Gal. 5:15).

B.   Speaking evil to each other (James 4:11).

C.   Suing a Christian or taking another believer to court (1 Cor. 6:7).

D.   Provoking or being envious of one another (Gal. 5:21).

E.   Judging or condemning each other (Rom. 14:13). This is not the same as judgement in the family or Church (1 Pet. 4:17). These are instances of righteous judgement.

F.   Infidelity and being unfaithful to each other (Gal. 5:19).

G.   Having dissension in the family (Gal. 5:20).

WE ALSO NEED A LIFESTYLE OF COMMITMENT TO THE LOCAL CHURCH

A.   Commitment is demonstrated by being in a specific Church family (Ps. 68:6, 92:12-15).
       The Local Church is like an umbrella over us, protecting us from Satan's arrows and harm (Ps. 91:1-6; Prov. 1:33). Peter warned the Early Church, "Save yourselves from this corrupt generation", and three thousand were added to the Church (Acts 2:40-41).

THE LOCAL CHURCH
protection against Satan's arrows

B.   Commitment is demonstrated by sharing burdens with the Church family (Acts 2:44-47).

C.   Commitment is demonstrated by supporting the vision of the Leaders and not having our own vision which only creates multivision: it means being under the authority of the Church Leaders (Heb. 13:17).

D.   We give our time and energy to that Church family: remember, the Local Church is mentioned 90% of the time in the Bible, and the Universal Church only 10%. So we emphasise what the Lord emphasises.

E.   Our financial support is given to the Local Church family (Mal. 3:10).

F.   We commit ourselves to the gatherings of that Church (Heb. 10:25).

G.   We verbally commit ourselves, which confirms our intentions (Josh. 24:15; Ruth 1:16). It is like making a marriage vow. We stay with each other through good and bad.

Like a natural family, children have one set of parents and live in one home. They would seem to be odd children if they said that they belonged to a worldwide family. So it is in Church. We are committed to one spiritual family, this principle making a Church healthy and secure.

CHAPTER 23
MEMBERS OF THE CHURCH

23. MEMBERS OF THE CHURCH

When the Early Church was established, and many became believers, scripture tells us that they were 'added' to their number (Acts 2:41, 47 and 5:14). 'Added' is from the Latin *addere*, meaning 'to join one thing to another', or 'to put together'.

A.   Jesus Himself confirmed that when we come together, He comes into that group and we can believe for great things to happen (Matt. 18:19-20).

B.   Paul talked about a group as defined in 1 Cor. 14:26.

C.   So it is understood that the Church is meant to be exclusive, based on certain conditions. The Greek word *ekklesia* or 'called-out ones' means 'citizens of that city whose citizenship is in Heaven (Phil. 3:20).

D.   Although membership is exclusive, attendance is open to all (James 2:2-4).

E.   To accept someone who is not a believer would contradict scripture. We can be members only by: faith (Mark 1:14-15); new birth (John 3:1-15); obedience (Matt. 7:21); endurance (Luke 9:62); repentance (Matt. 3:2); humility and sacrifice (Matt. 19:14-24).

THE NEW TESTAMENT CHURCH KNEW WHO WERE WITH THEM

A.   Jesus had twelve Apostles who were named and numbered (Luke 9:1 and 12).

B.   There were seventy others that Jesus chose (Luke 10:1-2).

C.   Five hundred were together when Jesus ascended to Heaven (1 Cor. 15:3-8).

D.   One hundred and twenty gathered in the upper room to seek the Holy Spirit (Acts: 1:15).

E.   Five thousand were added to the Church (Acts 4:4).

F.   They knew exactly who the disciples were (Acts 6:7).

WHAT DOES SCRIPTURE SAY ABOUT RECORDING MEMBERS' NAMES?

A.   Jesus gave a principle of a shepherd knowing who his sheep are (John 10:3-6 and 14). If a Pastor does not know who his sheep are, it is impossible to pastor them.

B.   Jesus clearly depicts those who are goats and those who are sheep (Matt. 25:31-35).

C.   The Israelites had their numbers recorded (Num. 1 and 2).

D.   The Levites were also recorded (Num. 3).

E.   When Israel left Babylon, the people were recorded in a book entitling them to minister in the priesthood (Ezra 2:3-60; Neh. 7).

F.   The Church of the Firstborn have their names written in Heaven (Heb. 12:22-24).

G.   All the redeemed are recorded in the Book of Life (Phil. 4:3; Rev. 13:8, 17:8, 20:12-15, 21:7). So spiritually and practically, the principle of recording names is clearly shown in scripture. Paul's letters reflect the stability of membership by listing individuals by name.

WHAT MAKES A MEMBER OF THE CHURCH?

Today's Church has been greatly weakened by those who are not accountable to anyone. This is not God's way. The only time in the New Testament when we see individuals not belonging to a Local Church was when they had been disciplined by the Leaders of that Church (Matt. 18:17; Titus 3:10).

A.   Membership is not based on having the same doctrine or signing a form. The first condition is believing on the Lord (Acts 5:14, 11:24; Rom. 10:9-10).

B.   There must be a practical expression of membership: believers are not only added to the Lord, but also to the Church (Acts 2:41-47).

C.   In the Bible, we are taught that we are part of both the Universal Church and the Local Church (1 Cor. 1:9).

D.   We also enjoy fellowship with each other (1 John 1:3 and 6-7). If we reject those Christ has sent, we reject Christ Himself.

E.   In the New Testament, membership could be transferred with letters of recommendation. If this was practised today, it would save the Church from a great deal of harm (Acts 18:27; Rom. 16:1; Col. 4:10). This would cure people from just drifting in.

F.   We cannot expect to receive all the benefits of the Church without being fully committed and taking up our responsibilities.

SOME HAVE DIFFICULTY WITH MEMBERSHIP FOR VARIOUS REASONS

A.   Not wanting_____ because they have independent spirits.

B.   They are_____ and do not like authority.

C.   They have been_____ in the past through abuse of membership.

D.   They are_____ and cannot take instruction.

E.   They have no_____ and they are not concerned about having it.

F.   They would be_____ from using their gifts in the way they desire.

THE BENEFITS OF MEMBERSHIP

A.   It is a protection against_____ (Prov. 11:1, 20:23).

B.   It gives a greater_____ of the mystery of God (Col. 2:2).

C.   It offers a greater release of God's_____ in gatherings (Matt: 18:19-20).

D.   It provides a greater_____ and a sense of belonging (1 Cor. 12:12-27).

E.   We produce greater_____ (Ps. 1:3, 46:4, 92:12-14; Is. 61:3; Eph. 4:16).

F.   There is_____ amongst the members (Gal. 6:1-2).

G.   It produces personal_____ from pastoral care and oversight (1 Thess. 5:12).

The Local Church is the instrument God uses to equip His people and to affect the world with the Gospel of the Good News of Christ. Every believer should be part of a Local Church. If we say no to the Local Church, we are in effect saying no to Jesus Christ and His eternal plan. We need each other to fulfil the call and plan of God on our lives.

So many have used the Church as a club: when they tire of it, they simply go to another. In Arizona, they have a weed called a tumbleweed: it never produces fruit because it has no roots. The same principle applies to those not rooted in a Church.

In Ps. 27:4, David said, "One thing I ask of the Lord, this is what I seek, that I may dwell in the House of the Lord all the days of my life, to gaze upon the beauty of the Lord and to seek Him in His temple."

"I love the House where You live, O Lord, the place where Your glory dwells" (Ps. 26:8). "In the great assembly I will praise the Lord" (Ps. 26:12).

In Heb. 2:12, Jesus proclaims, "In the presence of the congregation I will sing Your praises." So in our gatherings, sometimes we might just hear Jesus sing our praises when we are planted in the House of the Lord.

CHAPTER 24
THE BODY OF CHRIST

24. THE BODY OF CHRIST

If every believer could grasp the understanding that he or she has a function, purpose or ministry that no-one else can fulfil, and that includes Pastors, Elders and the congregation, then the Church, the very Body of Christ, would be transformed beyond all recognition. Individuals can do what the Pastor or Elders cannot: even famous names cannot do what God has called individuals to do in His Body.

Rom. 12:1-5 encourages us, "I urge you, brothers, in view of God's mercy, to offer your bodies as living sacrifices, holy and pleasing to God – this is your spiritual act of worship. Do not conform any longer to the pattern of this world, but be transformed by the renewing of your mind. Then you will be able to test and approve what God's will is – His good, pleasing and perfect will. For by the grace given me I say to every one of you: Do not think of yourself more highly than you ought, but rather think of yourself with sober judgement, in accordance with the measure of faith God has given you. Just as each of us has one body with many members, and these members do not all have the same function, so in Christ we who are many form one Body, and each member belongs to all the others."

THE CHURCH OF THE BODY OF CHRIST HAS ONE HEAD – JESUS CHRIST (EPH. 5:23)

A. Christ is the source of life to the Body (Col. 1:18, 2:10-13).

B. Christ is the sustainer of the life of the Body (Col. 2:19).

C. Christ is the sovereign authority in the Church (Eph. 5:23-24).

D. The Church as the Body of Christ has many members (1 Cor. 12:20).

E. All the members are directed by the Head (Eph. 1:21-22, 4:15-16).

F. All of us have been joined together through Christ (Eph. 2:13; 1 Cor. 12:13).

G.   Independence is not part of God's design (1 Cor. 12:21-22 and 26).

H.   We are all vital parts of the Body (1 Cor. 12:27).

GOD HAS GIVEN US NATURAL TALENTS

A.   Each of us has a talent that is of benefit to the whole (1 Cor. 12:28).

B.   Talents, such as using our hands or running our businesses, are to be used for God's glory (Matt. 25:14-20).

GOD HAS GIVEN US SPIRITUAL GIFTS

A.   Spiritual gifts are also to be used for the benefit of the whole Body (1 Cor. 12:7 and 11).

B.   Christ pours Himself into us and we reflect Him (Col. 1:27). One phrase we hear regularly today is, 'my ministry': it is not 'mine', nor do we own the gifts Christ has given us. We have them on loan to build His Church and His Kingdom, and we are not meant to place ownership on the gifts.

C.   Working together, all the gifting reveals the fullness of Christ (Eph. 1:22-23).

The Body of Christ, which is the Church, is very important to God. So anything we do to the Church, we actually do to Christ Jesus. If we withhold our tithes from the Church, God says we rob Him. <u>Why?</u> It is because the Church is God's visible expression on Earth (Mal. 3:8-9). If we attack individuals in the Church, we attack Jesus Christ. Saul attacked the Church in Acts 8:3, he went from house to house persecuting it. In Acts 9:5, God spoke to Saul. He did not ask why he was persecuting the Church but asked why he was persecuting <u>Him</u>. So a low commitment to the Church is a low commitment to Jesus.

CHURCH MEMBERS DEPEND ON EACH OTHER

A.   Members of the Body are all members of each other (1 Cor. 12:7-27).

B.   Members of the Body seek to encourage and strengthen each other (Rom. 14:19).

C.   Members of the Body must do all they can to live with each other (Mark 9:50).

D.   Members of the Body must have the interests of others at heart (Heb. 10:24-25).

HOW DO I FIND MY PLACE IN THE BODY?

A.   No gifting is more_____ than another (1 Cor. 12:21-25).

B.   See which area you have been called to_____ in (1 Cor. 12:27-31).

C.   All giftings_____ over time. We are to seek the gifts that build the Church, not to specialise in any particular one (1 Cor. 12:31).

D.   We are to_____ use our gifts and lay down our will (Rom. 12:1-2 and 10).

E.   We each have a specific place to function and are_____ for it before the Lord (1 Cor. 12:9, 11 and 18).

F.   Whatever gift we have, it has been loaned to us so we can_____ the Body of Christ (Luke 22:26-27).

G.   Our giftings are to be_____ to Christ Jesus (Eph. 1:21-23, 4:15, 5:23).

H.   It is the Lord who equips us with_____ to build His Church (Rom. 12:3-6; 1 Pet. 4:10).

I.   It is the Lord who has_____ us for the giftings He has given us (Eph. 2:10).

J.   It is the_____ of God that enables us to do His work (Phil. 2:13).

K.   Whatever gift we have, it is for the_____ of others (1 Cor. 10:24).

L.   Whatever gift we have, it is all from the _____ _____ (1 Cor. 12:7-11).

If the Body of Christ flows together in unity toward the same goals, keeping Christ and not our desires at the head, then the Church will be effective and powerful: in fact, we can ask anything in the name of Jesus and we will be given it (John 14:13-14).

So with united hearts, let us move on to give all the glory to the Lord God (Rom. 6:5).

ANSWERS

CHAPTER 1

Puffs up

Loves

Learners

Stupid

Listen

Wiser

Delight

Pretend

Correction

Teacher

Sacrifice

Examine

CHAPTER 2

Deluded

Impression

Conviction

Tearful moments

Remorse

Resolution

Decision

Form

Who does good

Believe

Evil

Mouth

Rejoicing

CHAPTER 3

Dependent

Impossible

Live

Bible

The Heart

Mouth

Obedience

Truth

Reading

Action

Exercise

Avoid

CHAPTER 4

Immersion

Commanded

Repent

Believe

Identifies

New

Overcome

Washes

Put off

Dying

New beginning

New name

CHAPTER 5

Fellowship

Grieved

Promise

Power

Experience

Speak in tongues

Wonders

Seen and heard

Spoke in tongues

Not filled

Holy Spirit

Spoke in tongues

Power

Edify

All

Fire

Sign

Ask

CHAPTER 6

Not my will

Hands

Self-pity

Own eyes

Is the Lord's

Lord and Master

Taught

Respond

Corrected

Home

Family

Occupation

Possessions

Strong

Reflect

Others to follow

Minister

Well done

CHAPTER 7

Communion

Two directions

God-ward

Man-ward

Men will know

The two

Doctrine

Bad lifestyles

Eat

Keep company

CHAPTER 8

Pride

Pay

Hates

Pride

Ruined

Be sure

Happenings

Bad choices

Ourselves

Heart

To win

CHAPTER 9

Revelation

Set apart

Himself

Himself

Belonging

Holy

CHAPTER 9 *Cont.*

Foolishness

Chose

Tell him

Word

According

Joy

CHAPTER 10

Wedding supper

Table

Communion

Bread

Reclined

Broke it

Body

Vine

Blood

Examine

Remember

Appreciate

United

Deepening

Thanks

Revelation

CHAPTER 11

Managing

Lives

Time

Talents and abilities

Possessions

Finances

Humble

Lose it

Increase

Servant

Exalts

Humbles

Nothing

Servant

Exalted

CHAPTER 12

People

Abraham

ARE

Blood

One

Blessed

Idle

Account

Speak

Receive

Multitude

CHAPTER 13

Tenth

Law

Everything

Greed

Blessed

Others

Gave

Trouble

Give

100 times

Given

Generous

First fruit

All

First fruit

CHAPTER 13 *Cont.*

Steal

Curse

Cheerful

Sacrificially

Willingly

Thankfully

Generously

CHAPTER 14

Discipline

Dependent

Choice

Attitude

Cost

Risk

Commitment

Good

Bad

Planted

Unfaithful

Destroyed

Tooth

Harm

Nothing

Carefully

Mix

Seed

CHAPTER 15

Ability

Lied

Truth

God

Edify

Attitude

Part

Surrendered

Thirst

All

Pray

Proportion

Neglect

Pillar

Foundation

CHAPTER 16

Spirit

Truth

Rules

Restore

Spirit

Soul

Body

Praise

Fruit

Soul

Pants

All

Praise

CHAPTER 17

Lonely

Head

Head

Provider

Love

Honour

Prayers

Authority

Submissive

Hospitality

CHAPTER 17 *Cont.*

Train

Correct

Disciplined

Sins

Responsibility

Heritage

Reward

Crown

Obey

CHAPTER 18

Defined will

Ethnic

Protection

Family

Brother

Name

Building

Extension

Denomination

Sect

Individual

Holy

Overcome

Victorious

Stain

Wrinkle

Blemish

Meeting

CHAPTER 19

All

Judges

All

Counsellors

Teachers

Families

House

Lord

Worship

Outpouring

Salvation

Health

Healing

Latter

Herself

CHAPTER 20

Church

Rule

Elders

Plurality

Character

Experienced

Home

Order

Gifting

Skills

Rule

Humility

Protect

Shepherds

Examples

Instruct

Account

Joy

You

Regard

Financially

Pray

Double

CHAPTER 21

Two

Others

Church

Listen

Sinned

Restoration

Integrity

Blameless

Holy

Radiant

Training

Harvest

CHAPTER 22

Husbands and wives

Himself

Loneliness

Dependent

Members

CHAPTER 23

Accountability

Rebellious

Hurt

Unteachable

Understanding

Restricted

Imbalance

Understanding

Presence

Fulfilment

Fruit

Accountability

Growth

CHAPTER 24

Important

Function

Develop

Sacrificially

Responsible

Serve

Submitted

Gifts

Prepared

Benevolence

Good

Same spirit

BIBLIOGRAPHY

LEWIS, C.S. (1952) *Mere Christianity*, New York, Harper Collins Publishers

FINNEY, C.G. (1851) *Lectures on Systematic Theology*, London, William Tegg & Co

SCHEIDLER, B., IVERSON, D. & CONNER, K. J. (1976) *Principles of Church Life*, Portland, City Christian Publishing

SWANNELL, J. ET AL (1992) *Oxford Modern English Dictionary*, Oxford, New York, Athens, Auckland, Bangkok, Berlin, Bombay, Calcutta, Cape Town, Dar es Salaam Dehli, Florence, Hong Kong, Ibadan, Istanbul, Karachi, Kuala Lumpur, Madras, Madrid, Melbourne, Mexico City, Nairobi, Paris, Singapore, Taipei, Tokyo, Toronto, Oxford University Press

SIMPSON, C. (1974) *Making Disciples*, New Wine